Catholicism at the Millennium

Catholicism at the Millennium

THE CHURCH OF TRADITION
IN TRANSITION

Edited by

GERALD L. MILLER *and* WILBURN T. STANCIL

Rockhurst University Press
Kansas City, Missouri
2001

ISBN 1-886761-25-6 (cloth), 1-886761-26-4 (paper)

Printed in the United States of America
01 02 03 04 05   5 4 3 2 1
First edition

To our students at Rockhurst,
past, present, and future

CONTENTS

FOREWORD

Catholicism at the Millennium: The Church of Tradition in Transition mirrors the institution from which it emerges—Rockhurst University. For almost one hundred years, Rockhurst has been training men and women to serve God and others in the world. Solidly anchored in the 450-year Jesuit tradition, Rockhurst, like the Roman Catholic Church, strives to maintain its roots and yet reach out to the aspirations and discoveries of today and tomorrow.

The volume affords readers the opportunity to explore both the old and the new, as the Roman Catholic Church, the Church of tradition, transitions into the third Christian millennium. The book assembles the well-articulated views of representative faculty from a wide spectrum of academic fields and schools at Rockhurst. It underscores the complementary relationship between faith and reason, the community of humanity as an arena for the discovery of God and God's truth, the ethical dimension necessary for the proper use of knowledge, the justice and dignity due to all persons, and the life of service as a way of discovering one's true self.

I hope that this book will aid readers in their own reflection on the crucial issues facing Catholicism at the millennium.

EDWARD KINERK, S.J.
President, Rockhurst University
Kansas City, Missouri

PREFACE

In recent years, most American Catholic colleges and universities have confronted the difficult challenge of maintaining a strong Catholic identity in the face of a rapidly diversifying and increasingly secularized culture. Rockhurst University—itself a part of that introspective and engaging dialogue involving academy, Church, and culture—stakes out its identity not only as a Catholic university but additionally as a Jesuit university.

In the face of a long-term and continued decline in the number of Jesuits, we at Rockhurst University have discussed, debated, argued, reflected, meditated, and prayed on how we will nurture and grow our Ignatian character and identity. And though the faculty, administration, and staff have long been engaged in the work of identifying and embodying those qualities distinctive of a Roman Catholic and Jesuit institution of higher learning, new challenges are constantly surfacing in an ongoing task.

To that end, in the fall of 1999, the president of Rockhurst, Father Edward Kinerk, commissioned a group of faculty and administrators to propose additional ways in which the Catholic and Jesuit identity of the institution could not only be maintained but further developed in the coming years. This group of faculty and administrators focused on cultivating ways to foster Catholic and Jesuit values through the next cycle of changes in higher education.

As the group met, it soon became clear that a consensus was forming around the notion of establishing a permanent institute or center for Catholic studies. It was equally apparent that there was a strong desire to take some steps now, even if small steps, long before a full-fledged center could be developed and funded. Out of this desire for some immediate action grew a series of one-hour lectures on the state of the Roman Catholic Church at the millennium. From the perspective of such diverse areas as theology, philosophy, biology, economics, sociology, music, history, and language, the lecturers explored, in retrospect and in prospect, what it means for the Catholic Church to be both a Church of tradition and a Church in transition.

A vital part of the lecture series included the participation of students, faculty, staff, and interested people from the Kansas City community. Discussions following each lecture oftentimes continued beyond the appointed time, indicating that the series had launched an invigorating examination of issues surrounding the faith.

Students' written summaries and reflections provided evidence that the deep and sometimes complex arguments in the lectures were not lost on the students and that they were genuinely challenged to think about Catholicism in new ways. Many stated that this lecture series was the best exposure they had ever had to a mature and carefully considered discussion of issues affecting the Church. When students report that they are eager to recommend a course in Catholicism to their fellow students, something unique has indeed taken place!

As the lectures unfolded, it became apparent that the series should be captured for a larger audience than could attend the weekly sessions. This book is an outgrowth of that desire for an extended audience. It also represents the initial publication of the Rockhurst University Press.

In many ways, this book is a snapshot not only of the Roman Catholic Church at the millennium, but also of Rockhurst University and its tradition of scholarship emanating from the classroom. However, the ongoing debates today involving academy, church, and culture assure that this publication will be an important contribution not only to scholars and students but to the larger community of readers who are concerned with the crucial issues facing Catholicism today.

A special acknowledgment is due to Michael McDonald and Tom Turner, both of whom made presentations in the series, and to the students who took a chance on this pathbreaking course: Kristin Arthur, Robert Becker, Tom Dugan, Ryan Herman, Brian Ismert, Katie Kammerer, Drew Kupsky, Matthew

Lang, Mary Lewis, Brad McCormack, Corey McLain, Jeffrey Mollner, Heather Nease, Patrick Riordan, Jessica Schroeder, Shaun Walsh, Nick Wastler, and Tara Workman.

GERALD L. MILLER
WILBURN T. STANCIL
Feast of Pentecost

ONE
Faith and History

1

"Cold, Bare Ruined Choirs"?: Reflections on the Nature of Catholic History

Richard J. Janet

A FRAMED PHOTOGRAPH of a ruined English monastery hangs prominently in my home. The photo was taken by Peter Nugent, a colleague on the Rockhurst University faculty, and is entitled *Henry VIII's Legacy*. The picture elegantly conveys a sense of longing for a world gone by, a Catholic world of beauty, mystery, and faith, and a bitterness toward the greedy, philistine forces of modernism represented by the English reformers. In expressing nostalgia for his lost youth in Sonnet 73, Shakespeare evokes the same image of a ruined monastery:

> That time of year thou mayst in me behold
> When yellow leaves, or none, or few do hang
> Upon those boughs which shake against the cold,
> Bare ruined choirs where late the sweet birds sang.

Not coincidentally, Garry Wills borrowed Shakespeare's metaphor for the title of his study of the American Catholic Church in the 1960s, *Bare Ruined Choirs: Doubt, Prophecy, and Radical Religion*. Indeed, a sense of loss and decay permeates much of what may be called Catholic historiography, a tradition that often lingers on the decline and fall of a once triumphant faith and seeks to mine the past for a glimpse of "the world we have lost." Francesca Murphy describes this kind of scholarship as "a sort of deep-sea diving—searching for the lost Atlantis, the sunken nation of Christendom" (Caldecott and Morrill 124).

Triumph and Decline in the History
of the Catholic Church

Examples of a "triumph and decline" model, including some excellent scholarship, abound in Catholic historiography. Eusebius chronicled the victory of Christianity over imperial Roman persecution; Lord Acton analyzed the agonies of a Church beset by a new variant of Roman authoritarianism. Bede narrated the story of the Church's triumph in Saxon England; Philip Hughes wrote of its demise in Tudor England. David Knowles celebrated the accomplishments of medieval Christendom; Roger Aubert reviewed the Church's declining influence in a secularizing society. John Tracy Ellis recorded the rise of an American Catholic Church; Garry Wills sounded the dirge for that Church in the turbulent 1960s and 1970s. Chapter titles from Thomas Bokenkotter's popular history of Catholicism reflect the rhetoric of triumph and decline historiography: "The Final Victory over Paganism," "The Decline of the Papal Monarchy," "The Catholic Church Recovers Its Spiritual Elan," "The French Revolution Shatters the Church of the Old Order," and "The Bark of Peter in Stormy Seas" (Bokenkotter iv–v).

Even one of the most celebrated works of Catholic revisionist history in recent times, Eamon Duffy's *The Stripping of the Altars: Traditional Religion in England, 1400–1580,* falls into the triumph and decline category. Duffy interprets often overlooked evidence on late-medieval English popular religion to assert that, contrary to prevailing historical opinion, the English people clung to religious sensibilities and forms that were both vibrant and consistent with elite, clerical religious forms. The rituals and liturgies of medieval Catholicism continued to influence English popular religion in the fifteenth and sixteenth centuries, according to Duffy, and, therefore, the well-known story of the English Reformation as a protracted but popular revolt against a decadent religious tradition must be revised (Duffy 4–5). Duffy's theme is a powerful one, communicated in an elegant prose style and substantiated by a careful reconstruction of late-medieval English popular religion based on important sources neglected by previous historians. But, as Francesca Murphy recognizes (Caldecott and Morrill 124), the argument remains essentially that of Hilaire Belloc, who sought to undermine the Henrician reformers at an elite level through disparaging biographies. Duffy, by far the more careful and diplomatic historian, merely adds an aesthetic dimension to Belloc's central argument. Both seek to rescue something of value from the "bare ruined choirs" of Tudor Catholicism. Both seek to explain the decline of a once-triumphant ecclesiastical and liturgical tradition in England.

I am, perhaps, ignoring the subtleties of these rightly acclaimed and highly nuanced historical works by assigning them to a crudely delineated triumph and decline category of interpretation. There may be good reasons, some of which I outline below, for approaching the history of Catholicism in the manner of these master historians. Their influence is difficult to escape— note the recent attempt by two English historians, one Catholic and one Protestant, to step outside the boundaries and offer a "radical interpretation" of the Reformation that discards the rhetoric of "us and them," victory and defeat. However, the resulting analysis, relying as it does on a natural metaphor of ebb and flow, is but a variation on the dominant theme (Fernandez-Armesto and Wilson x). The fact remains that much Church history shares to some degree in the language of triumph and decline, and focuses on the fortunes of institutional Catholicism and its manifestations. As a body of literature, the works I have mentioned make up a distinguished canon and compare favorably with the scholarship of any tradition. But does this approach constitute, in toto, the definition of "Catholic history"? I think not.

The triumph and decline approach to the history of Catholicism does offer attractive advantages to the historian. It is a simple, elegant model for tracking the history of human institutions with a tradition stretching back to the cyclical historical notions of the classical historians. Indeed, as a discipline focused on the incidence and nature of change, history relies on stories of the rise and fall of individuals, groups, societies, ideas, and cultures. And for the Christian historian, the triumph and decline approach offers a comforting reaffirmation of the cycle of life and death, decay and resurrection, sin and redemption. St. Augustine's *City of God*, the foundational work of the Christian philosophy of history, reminded Romans that only the Heavenly City was permanent—all Earthly Cities, even Rome, were temporal and subject to inevitable corruption and death. More recently, the English Catholic historian Christopher Dawson provided another possible argument for the triumph and decline model in his correlation of religion and culture. If religion and culture are inseparable, as he insisted, then every era of human cultural decline (which Augustine saw as inevitable) is also an era of religious decline. Indeed, for Dawson, the decline of religion defined the decline of culture and vice versa.

But the seductiveness of the triumph and decline model and of its claim as the sole criterion for "Catholic history" is lessened in the face of religious argument and historical reality. As a human institution, religion is a primary component of culture, but religion is that part of culture that seeks to link with the Heavenly City. Religion has a spiritual core, and Catholic Christianity has a fundamental transcendent quality. Unless one is willing to define religion as solely a social construct, one must accept that religion might in some respects transcend human culture. Thus, religion might survive the rise and fall of empires, as Christianity survived the fall of Rome. Some early modern philosophers were, indeed, willing to dismiss Christianity as mere superstition, albeit on a grand scale, and some modern ideologues defined religion as a psychosocial phenomenon. Edward Gibbon and Karl Marx are their historians. Catholic historians seek a fuller, deeper appreciation of the nature of faith and religion.

By way of an historical example, imagine the following historical scenario: a civilization in transition with the prevailing political order threatened by "barbarian" forces from without and by civic and moral corruption from within; a Church, part and parcel of this threatened civilization, split by theological divisions and subject to harsh attacks for its failure to stem the rising tide of barbarism; a towering intellect, heavily involved in the intellectual controversies of the day, seeking to provide answers for this troubled age through his calls for a spiritual reinterpretation of history and culture. What era and individual does this scenario describe? St. Augustine in the fifth-century Roman Empire? Or Christopher Dawson in twentieth-century Europe? Of course, this brief portrait could describe either era or either individual. Are both eras, then, ages of decline? Can historians find a period that was not an age of decline, based on one set of criteria or another? If not, is the language of triumph and decline rendered meaningless? Is civilization in a constant state of rise and fall, *corso ricorso*, so that history becomes the chronicle of "one damned thing after another"? Or has civilization constantly spiraled downward, as Hesiod and the ancient Greeks suggested? Surely the answers to these questions should reflect something of the faith of the historian. The faith of the historian tempers his historical imagination. Christianity is a religion of hope, made possible by Christ's act of redemption. As such, there is a purpose to history—even the history of the Earthly City. That purpose and that act of historical imagination enable us to speak of a "Catholic history."

Roots of a Catholic History

The thought of St. Augustine is fundamental to any reconstruction of a Christian philosophy of history. Augustine's concept of the two cities and of the relationship between the two gives human history meaning and purpose. The Heavenly City is eternal and the goal of all Christians, who are but sojourners in the Earthly City. The Earthly City is temporal and prone to decay and corruption, but the Christian owes an allegiance to that city and is responsible for good citizenship so that, however imperfectly, it reaches out to the heavens. The things of the earth are flawed by human sin but remain good gifts of God and may be studied so as to improve life and to offer something of the divine intelligence. Augustine gave meaning to the passage of history and offered purpose in the final realization of the Heavenly City.

Christopher Dawson offers a twentieth-century complement to Augustine's historical thought. Dawson exercised a tremendous influence on the Western intellectual arena from 1930 through the 1950s. Born of an affluent family in rural England in 1889, educated at Winchester and Trinity College, Oxford, he converted to Catholicism in 1914. An inspiring visit to Rome in 1909 (during which, like Edward Gibbon two centuries earlier, he resolved to write a sweeping history of culture), marriage into a prominent English Catholic family, and close study of Catholic literature contributed to his conversion (Allitt 244). Like Arnold Toynbee and Oswald Spengler, after World War I Dawson wrote broad histories of the rise and fall of civilizations, although from the beginning he emphasized "spiritual factors and the element of free will in the creation and preservation of a culture" (Allitt 245). In works such as *Progress and Religion* (1929) and *The Making of Europe* (1932), he demonstrated his wide erudition and detailed knowledge of ancient and medieval civilizations, using the techniques of modern historical research, anthropology, and archaeology.

Throughout his career, the major themes of Dawson's works revolved around the importance of religion in human culture and the particular influence of Christianity on Western civilization. Even secular reviewers, normally wary of "Catholic" histories, praised Dawson's learning and sensitivity, and Dawson was usually careful to avoid oversimplification in his treatment of modernist thinkers who denied the essential role of religion in human history (Allitt 254). Dawson's reputation grew in the 1940s, when he was invited to deliver the prestigious Gifford Lectures at the University of Edinburgh (later published as *Religion and Culture* and *Religion and the Rise of Western Culture*). In 1958, he came to the United States to assume the newly created chair of Catholic studies at Harvard University. Four years later, Dawson returned to England, where he died in 1970. He lost much of his intellectual influence in the 1960s, when historians rejected his sweeping, synthetic histories in favor of detailed analyses of narrow populations devoid of moral judgment. But Christopher Dawson's widely acknowledged mastery of broad historical fields and especially his insistence on the linkage between religion and culture have deeply influenced attempts to define Catholic history.

What Augustine and Dawson suggest is that Catholic history is not merely the history of Catholicism or the history of any specific topic per se. Augustine wondered whether Eusebius's history of the early Church was an appropriate venture. Dawson was certainly interested in the history of the Church and in the history of religious sensibilities in general, but he incorporated that interest into his vision of a metahistory that combined all aspects of human culture—religion being, of course, a primary component of that culture. Both men's works focus on the "big picture"—Augustine on the fall of Rome and the decline of earthly empires in general, Dawson on the rise of European culture and on its precarious position in the middle of the twentieth century. Both historians exercised their Catholic Christianity as an act of moral imagination that tempered their approaches to their broad topics. Theoretically, then, following Augustine and Dawson, the Catholic historian should be able to write about any historical topic and should bring to that topic not a prescribed method or model but a cultivated imagination able to place all events in a "Catholic" perspective.

ELEMENTS OF A CATHOLIC HISTORY

The elements of a Catholic history follow from the long tradition of Catholic thought, especially from theology and philosophy. Like all Catholic intellectual endeavors, Catholic history presupposes the pursuit of truth as the ultimate goal of historical inquiry and recognizes the ultimate harmony between faith and reason. Specifically, Catholic history reflects four basic perspectives on the nature of human events: an overarching providentialism, the primacy of free will, the confluence of faith and culture, and the ultimate meaning that links human events throughout history.

Providentialism

Providence has become an antiquated term that the modern reader confronts mainly in the novels, letters, and memoirs of Victorian authors and statesmen. In its broadest sense, Providence refers to the benign ordering of human events. For the Christian, Providence refers specifically to God's foresight and God's shaping and directing of history. In the modern era, secular theories of progress and development have replaced references to Providence. Robert Nisbet credits Augustine with formulating a Christian concept of change and development guided by "the will of omnipotent God." Augustine's definition of Providence proved irresistible to later philosophers of history and social theorists, who, Nisbet suggests, "would modify the Augustinian vision and, especially after the seventeenth century, secularize it; placing in 'nature,' 'spirit,' 'civilization,' or 'dialectic' what they took from the God whom Augustine had made responsible for the First Principle." "As a First Cause," Nisbet concludes, "God would in time disappear, his place taken by one or other of the secular determinisms of the eighteenth and nineteenth centuries" (Nisbet 64).

In *Progress and Religion*, Christopher Dawson considered the displacement of Providence in favor of the modern idea of progress evidence of the decadence of modern culture. Modern theories of progress retain the providential notion of an ultimate ordering of human affairs but balk at the consequences of belief in an overarching spiritual reality. Theorists of progress strive to overcome the embarrassment of faith and the difficulties of reconciling belief in a loving, omnipotent God with the intricacies of natural processes. Catholics have traditionally understood Providence as follows: God is the ultimate cause and goal of everything, but God works through secondary causes to respect human free will and to allow the consequences of human choice. God works through secondary causes by always being present in human history (McBrien 324).

Of course, an unabashed belief in Providence raises potential problems for the Catholic historian. Dermot Quinn identifies the problem: "[The Catholic historian] must make a case for design, also for divine purpose enshrined in it. This is possible, but the messiness of history often gets in the way" (Caldecott and Morrill 73). A simplistic application of the influence of Providence leaves historians open to charges of bias and naïveté. It is, therefore, imperative for Catholic historians to master the "messiness" of history and to understand the complexities of Providence. But they should not apologize for their beliefs. All historians come to their works with some beliefs or values, often as not what amounts to secularized versions of Providence— that is, belief in progress, fate, the logic of history, or the realization of an Absolute Idea. And belief in Providence does not absolve the historian from a close analysis of secondary causes. It does impose, perhaps, a special obligation to balance history and theology and to recognize the limitations of both modes of inquiry. When that balance is lost, the Catholic historian does neither his faith nor his profession credit. Jacques Bossuet, the eighteenth-century French bishop who attempted a reconstruction of human events drawn from "the very words of Scriptures," is often cited as a historian who forsook history for theology (Caldecott and Morrill 73).

Freedom of the Will

Acceptance of an overarching Providence is joined, for the Catholic historian, to belief in the primacy of free will in human history, to the notion that humans are totally free "and at the same time grounded in the grace and presence of God" (McBrien 325). Human choice is the drivespring of history, not totalitarian structures or predetermined political or economic ends. This notion seems particularly quaint at the beginning of the third millennium, when intellectuals analyze institutional trends or, if they do consider the human equation, look for universal archetypes. Twentieth-century governments understood the power of such forces and sought to herd individuals toward common, statist goals. Christopher Dawson recognized this tendency but determinedly clung to a humanist interpretation of history.

> But in spite of the modern totalitarian tendency to control the development of culture by the external methods of legislation and internal organization and the control of parties and political police, it is still the individual mind that is the creative force which determines the fate of cultures. And the first step in the transformation of culture is a change in the pattern of culture within the mind, for this is the seed out of which there springs new forms of life which ultimately change the social way of life and thus create new culture. (*Historic Reality* 20)

The events of 1989–90 in central Europe seem to confirm Dawson's assertions, as seemingly spontaneous individual acts stemming from changes "in the pattern of culture within the mind" transformed previously communist cultures. Indeed, Timothy Garton Ash explains the revolutions of 1989 in just such terms in *The Magic Lantern: The Revolution of '89 Witnessed in Warsaw, Budapest, Berlin, and Prague.*

For the Catholic historian, then, history is a story of human choices and their consequences in the context of an overarching Providence. The works of Marvin R. O'Connell—my teacher, friend, and mentor at the University of Notre Dame—provide a clear example of this fundamental element of Catholic history. Over a forty-year period, O'Connell has written about some of the most controversial events, figures, and ideas in the history of modern Western religion and thought. From the Spanish Inquisition to the Catholic modernist movement, from the Counter-Reformation to the Oxford Movement, from Blaise Pascal to John Ireland, O'Connell has published stylish narratives that accept events as the product of human choices, and he interprets them without an overriding bias or predetermined theory (although, of course, he is sometimes accused of bias, given the controversial nature of his topics). He once proudly repeated the words of a critic who claimed he could not tell whether O'Connell's book on the Counter-Reformation, published in the Norton *Rise of Modern Europe* series, was written by a Catholic or a Protestant. O'Connell offers clear, compelling stories of important and hotly debated topics based on the premise that before one ventures a judgment on any issue (especially a controversial one), it is imperative to know that issue well. I recall a story O'Connell told about a young priest at a cocktail party who tried to offer an opinion on John Henry Newman, starting with "I don't know much about Newman, but . . ." "Stop," O'Connell cried, "if you don't know about him, then it is better not to speak at all."

Marvin O'Connell answers those critics who complain that a Catholic perspective hopelessly biases a historian, as in this passage from an article on the Spanish Inquisition:

> But perhaps the Spanish Inquisition was indeed a wicked institution. If so, that judgment should be made on the basis of those discernible facts an honest examination is able to reveal, and not upon the fevered testimony of self-interested politicians, biased preachers, witless pamphleteers, or—deriving from one or more of these—naïve writers of fiction. And, as is the case with any historical reconstruction of a phenomenon now passed away, to understand the contextual framework is a condition for understanding the phenomenon itself. ("Spanish Inquisition" 7)

Perhaps, O'Connell implies, what angers secular historians is less how Catholic historians do their work than their choice of topics and their politics.

In addition to his central emphasis on history as the story of human choices and their consequences, Marvin O'Connell provides other examples for Catholic historians. His interests are broad and varied, and belie the prevailing academic environment of hyperspecialization. I once submitted a paper to him that reviewed a biography of the nineteenth-century English statesmen Lord Palmerston. I noted in the review that the biographer had written an earlier biography of the sixteenth-century English churchman Thomas Cranmer and questioned the biographer's competence to venture into the murky waters of Victorian politics given that he was "a sixteenth-century man." Little did I know at the time of O'Connell's own broad interests and publications, so he, of course, rightly chastised me for my academic snobbery.

Finally, Marvin O'Connell insists on well-written histories. His own elegant prose and storytelling ability led him to publish a novel (*McElroy*) about American Catholicism in the 1970s. In his respect for the primacy of free will and the distinctiveness of human events, as well as in his storytelling approach and abilities, his insistence on thorough grounding in the topic and knowledge of the issues, his eclectic and ecumenical interests, and his gift for clear and elegant communication, Father Marvin R. O'Connell models the virtues of the Catholic historian.

The Confluence of Faith and Culture

If God works through secondary causes to shape and direct history, or, to put it another way, if history results from the free choices of human beings under an overarching Providence, the Catholic historian is faced with the task of finding God in the drama of human history. Amidst the "messiness" of history, the Catholic historian seeks to recognize the spiritual moment through which Providence works in a material world. Again, according to Francesca Murphy, "the mark of a Catholic history is the description of a lifting up of natural human beings and human culture by and toward Christian spirit. A Catholic historian captures this moment of moral transformation. He is one who can imagine historical events as being to some extent infused with a Christian charism" (Caldecott and Morrill 126). This is the Catholic version of the problem facing all working historians in one form or another—understanding the relationship between the general and the specific, between the major themes and the supporting details. Any coherent historical perspective requires a definition and delineation of these points, or history becomes a mere chronicle of disconnected events. Recognition of the key event, the most significant moment, or the overwhelming trend gives purpose to history. Without it, interpretation becomes impossible, and history textbooks would fill reams of paper and whole wings of libraries.

Augustine suggested that human beings exist at the junction of the material and the spiritual, the Earthly and Heavenly Cities. Human beings reside in the Earthly City but are sojourners, pilgrims journeying toward the ultimate reality of the Heavenly City. The Earthly City is necessarily real and not, as some postmodernists would have it, a fleeting construct of human imagination or invention. Living in this very real realm, humans create cultures through the exercise of their free will, but these cultures are infused with the spiritual and cannot be understood without reference to religion, a point Christopher Dawson constantly made. Human culture cannot be anything but material and spiritual at the same time, for human beings carry the spark of the Heavenly City with them on Earth.

For the historian, this means that all human events may be studied empirically without sacrificing a sense of the general purpose of history. Human events become, as it were, artifacts of the spiritual working in the material world. Thus, Catholic historians may rightly study any human activity and study it rigorously and scientifically, while respecting the providential sweep of history. In a real way, the general themes of history are revealed in the specific acts of human beings, which build toward recognition of an ultimate spiritual reality.

Ultimate Purpose

Finally, Catholic history must be regarded as a vertical rather than a horizontal process. Catholic historians seek a thorough understanding of the context of every event and every era, but they do so while connecting each event to the chain of events preceding and following it. John Morrill explores this theme in his contribution to a book of essays commemorating the work of Christopher Dawson:

> Vertical history is that which discards the dross of the particular and the contingent—the prejudices, blindnesses and contentions of an age—in order to extract the residual gold, the truth and insight of enduring value. . . . Horizontal history resolutely sets out to place each event, idea, institution in its contemporary contexts. It seeks out not the enduring, the survival of the fittest idea, but rather the contingent and the ordinary in the context of time. The vertical approach emphasizes the continuity of past and present; the horizontal approach, as William Lamont has it, "can serve best by restoring a sense of inaccessibility." (Caldecott and Morrill 4)

Catholic history seeks the continuities in history because it recognizes a central human event—the Incarnation—as the spiritual tie binding past, present, and future. The Venerable Bede understood this spiritual tie in the seventh century when he popularized the practice of ordering human history around the birth of Christ (hence B.C. and A.D.). Bede's practice has given way today to the fashion of denigrating the central event of the Incarnation in favor of a recognition of the rise of a (for better or worse) Christian era (hence B.C.E. and C.E.), or, for some, a secularized "common era." What used to be considered metahistories—histories that sought a linkage between past and present, including the histories of Renaissance humanists who looked for threads connecting their era to the classical past, the works of early modern historians such as Voltaire and Gibbon, who were extremely sensitive to evidence of cultural continuities, and nineteenth-century Whig history—have become unfashionable today. Such histories are rejected as "presentist" and ahistorical, and are derided for their failure to understand the complexities of human events. But, as I have noted, Catholic historians wed this concern for continuity with an emphasis on history as the story of human choice and on finding the spiritual in the material, thereby obligating them to do the hard work of analyzing each historical event on its own merits before blindly linking it to a broader pattern.

The case of Alfred Noyes in the first half of the twentieth century provides an interesting glimpse of an attempt to synthesize apparently contradictory trends and elements. Noyes was a famous English poet of a traditional bent (he is best known for his poem *The Highwayman*) who converted to Catholicism and wrote essays seeking the spiritual in a material world. He composed a series of poems on the early modern scientists, attempting to reconcile perceived tensions between science and religion, and wrote a biography of Voltaire positing that the notorious Enlightenment deist was actually not far from orthodox Christianity in his beliefs. The leading intellectuals of his day of course derided Noyes for his unfashionable poetry and his efforts to revise the comfortable notions of secular progress to which Western thought had grown accustomed.

CONCLUSION

A review of the elements of a genuinely Catholic history—a history marked by acceptance of Providence and human free will, by the attempt to find the spiritual amidst the complexity of material events, and by efforts to link events vertically around the central fact of the Incarnation—leads to a recognition that Catholic history cannot be defined as a single method, approach, or topical focus. Catholic history is not necessarily denominational history or ecclesiastical history or historical theology, much less religious history written from a prevailing perspective of "triumph and decline." Catholic historians write about events across the wide spectrum of human activity, geography, and chronology, and they employ the methods of the most rigorous scientific, empirical studies of the past. Catholic history may best be defined as a sensibility toward the past or, better yet, a cultivated sense of moral imagination: cultivated in its demand for hard work and constant attention, moral in its recognition of the spiritual underpinnings and purpose of earthly existence, and imaginative in its efforts to find the common elements linking events across time and cultures.

Why pursue a Catholic history in the third millennium, when the prevailing intellectual culture dismisses such moral exercise of the mind as a quaint remnant of a superstitious age gone by? The maintenance of a Catholic Christian history is important because history remains central to the Christian experience and because some, taking advantage of the Christian appreciation of history, would distort our understanding of the past to promote an apocalyptic or utopian vision. Catholic history is important because, as Pope John Paul II reminds us, "For the people of God . . . history becomes a path to be followed to the end, so that by the unceasing action of the Holy Spirit the contents of revealed truth may find their full expression" (John Paul II 20).

Works Cited

Allitt, Patrick. *Catholic Converts: British and American Intellectuals Turn to Rome*. Ithaca: Cornell University Press, 1997.

Augustine of Hippo. *The City of God against the Pagans*. Cambridge Texts in the History of Political Thought. Cambridge: Cambridge University Press, 1998.

Bokenkotter, Thomas. *A Concise History of the Catholic Church*. Revised and expanded edition. New York: Image, 1990.

Caldecott, Stratford, and John Morrill, eds. *Eternity in Time: Christopher Dawson and the Catholic Idea of History*. Edinburgh: T&T Clark, 1997.

Dawson, Christopher. *The Historic Reality of Christian Culture: A Way to the Renewal of Human Life*. New York: Harper and Bros., 1930.

———. *The Making of Europe: An Introduction to the History of European Unity*. London: Sheed and Ward, 1932.

———. *Progress and Religion: An Historical Enquiry*. New York: Sheed and Ward, 1929.

———. *Understanding Europe*. New York: Sheed and Ward, 1952.

Duffy, Eamon. *The Stripping of the Altars: Traditional Religion in England, 1400–1580*. New Haven: Yale University Press, 1992.

Fernandez-Armesto, Felipe, and Derek Wilson. *Reformations: A*

Radical Reinterpretation of Christianity and the World, 1500–2000. New York: Scribner, 1997.

Garton Ash, Timothy. *The Magic Lantern: The Revolution of '89 Witnessed in Warsaw, Budapest, Berlin, and Prague.* New York: Vintage, 1993.

John Paul II. *Fides et Ratio.* September 14, 1998.

McBrien, Richard P. *Catholicism.* 2 vols. Minneapolis: Winston, 1980.

Nisbet, Robert A. *Social Change and History: Aspects of the Western Theory of Development.* New York: Oxford University Press, 1970.

O'Connell, Marvin R. *Blaise Pascal: Reasons of the Heart.* Grand Rapids: W. B. Eerdmans, 1997.

———. *The Counter-Reformation, 1559–1610.* New York: Harper and Row, 1974.

———. *Critics on Trial: An Introduction to the Catholic Modernist Movement.* Washington, D.C.: Catholic University of America Press, 1995.

———. *John Ireland and the American Catholic Church.* St. Paul: Minnesota Historical Society, 1988.

———. *McElroy: A Novel.* New York: W. W. Norton, 1980.

———. *The Oxford Conspirators: A History of the Oxford Movement, 1833–1845.* New York: Macmillan, 1969.

———. "The Spanish Inquisition: Fact versus Fiction." *Catholic Dossier* 2, no. 6 (November–December 1996): 6–10.

Wills, Garry. *Bare Ruined Choirs: Doubt, Prophecy, and Radical Religion.* Garden City, N.Y.: Doubleday, 1972.

TWO
Truth and Belief

2

Reason and Religion at the Millennium

Brendan Sweetman

THE FOCUS OF my all too brief reflections in this chapter is delib-
erately broad so that I can concentrate on religious belief in general as a feature of human experience, particularly its interaction
with secularism and other trends in contemporary thought.
Later, I focus more specifically on some interesting features of
Catholicism in relation to the issues I have raised. My aim in this
chapter is to consider three interesting and timely questions: (1)
What is the state of reason at the millennium? (2) How has the
state of reason influenced religion at the millennium? and (3)
How is religion responding to and dealing with this influence?
These are very large questions, and I can do no more here in a
popular-style work than briefly outline my responses to them.

The Irish satirist Jonathan Swift once asked the question
whether man was a rational animal or just an *animal rationes
capax*, an animal capable of reason! Swift, with his misanthropic
view of the world, was inclined to answer this question in the
negative. He was motivated by the folly of humankind in a variety of fields, and his frustration at what he saw as our inability
to use reason sufficiently in our attempts to understand and live
in the world. Today, it is instructive to consider a deeper, more
philosophical question about reason: What is the state of reason
in the year 2000? In the first part of the chapter, I want to briefly
sketch my answer to this question.

THE STATE OF REASON AT THE MILLENNIUM

It is helpful to begin by sketching historically (in a very cursory
way) the role of reason in philosophy and in the history of ideas

generally. In the history of philosophy, the great thinkers—such as Plato, Aristotle, St. Augustine, St. Thomas Aquinas, and so on—regarded reason as the way to knowledge and truth. They understood truth to mean an account of how things really stood in the world, of what is really the case, of what really obtains. Truth was the ultimate goal of all human inquiry, and most philosophers believed one could obtain truth. In particular, they agreed that reason was adequate to this task—that it was within the power of human reason to discover the truth about things, big and small. They did not hold, of course, that we could find the complete truth on every single issue or that everyone would agree on what the truth is, but they did believe that in general truth was attainable and that there could be agreement on many issues. These great philosophers did not always agree among themselves on the various issues with which they were mutually concerned—the nature of reality, the nature of the human person, the nature of moral and political values, to name the main issues. Plato and Aristotle, for example, famously disagreed on the true account of reality; however, they did agree on the power of reason to know the real and on its general necessity in the lives of human beings. It was Aristotle who said, after all, that man is first and foremost a rational animal.

We must also emphasize that along with a belief in truth and a belief in the power of reason to discover truth, most traditional philosophers advanced a *realist* philosophy. Realism in philosophy is the view that the human mind can know reality as it really is in itself. Reality is outside the mind, and the mind can gain access to it in human knowledge; in particular, there is no significant distortion going on—by means of culture or language or concepts or gender or race or national identity—in the mind's grasp of reality. The dominant attitude was that reality presents itself to the mind and then *the mind conforms to it*, much as the film in a camera "conforms" to the image when it is exposed to it and which it accurately reflects.

This view was in the ascendancy in philosophy until the time of Descartes and his successors, when several philosophers (such as Locke and Kant) began to question the power of reason to know reality. At first glance, this questioning seems extremely odd. For how is it possible to attack or criticize reason in general? One can easily understand how one might attack a particular theory of truth (for example, Plato's theory of forms) or a particular moral claim (for example, Socrates' claim that no one does evil knowingly) or a particular metaphysical claim (for example, that God does not exist), but attacking *reason itself* might seem odd to the nonphilosopher. What were those philosophers who attacked reason trying to do? What was their motivation? Or to look at the issue from the other way around, what was so wrong with reason that philosophers began to call it into question?

One of the main motivations of these philosophers was the philosophical view known as antirealism, the view that the human mind cannot know reality as it really is in itself; all we can know is reality *as it appears to us* in human knowledge. Although Descartes did not propose this view, it had its modern origins in his work because of his famous arguments for skepticism and his failure, according to many philosophers, to refute these arguments. Descartes's approach was to be very influential in leading to Locke's antirealist tendencies. Antirealism first appeared seriously in the modern era with Locke's distinction between primary and secondary qualities, and reached its fullest expression in Kant's distinction between the phenomena and the noumena. However, it is clearly this line of thinking that is the forerunner of the contemporary view, in the ascendancy in many disciplines, that all knowledge is *contextual.* Whereas Locke argued that at least the primary qualities (solidity, extension, shape, and so on) were exempt from the modifications of the knowing mind and so objective knowledge of the primary qualities is possible, his general distinction between primary and secondary qualities (color, odor, flavor, sound, and so on) has evolved today into the view that it is language, culture, and tradition, perhaps even race and gender, that modify the objects of consciousness and, further and crucially, that these features of experience are responsible for modifying *all* the objects of consciousness. The result of this approach is that the search for so-called objective knowledge—for transcendental, transhistorical essences and truths—is an illusion because there are no such truths.

It is important to emphasize that the antirealist thinker is not

saying that the mind *produces* the world, for the world, according
to the antirealist, is there and exists independently of the mind.
But the world *as it is known in human knowledge and human experience*—the meaning of tables and chairs, of moral and political
values, of worldviews, of religions—is "produced" by human
beings. All of our mental representations, images, ideas, concepts—all mental content—are modified by certain features of
human experience, most notably culture, language, background
beliefs, and so on. And, crucially, this modifying is not trivial or
benign; antirealism involves the radical and controversial claim
that one cannot look at reality and know it in any kind of objective sense; one's looking at the world is always compromised in
important respects by the angle or viewpoint from which one is
doing the looking. It is not just that culture influences one's out-
look, which nobody would deny; it is the view that all claims
to knowledge are ineluctably compromised by the modifying
structures of the human mind (and various philosophers provide different accounts of these modifying structures—for example, Kant, Heidegger, Derrida).

Now this is what the antirealist *holds*. But illustrating or dem-
onstrating that these controversial claims are true or at least
plausible is quite another thing, and I do not think that anyone
has ever succeeded in showing that this view is plausible. In fact,
in contemporary thought, although antirealism is very popular,
there is seldom a serious attempt made to defend it or argue for
it and to try to illustrate its superiority over the realist alternative. Antirealism is simply an *assumption* of much contemporary
discourse in many disciplines; it is taken as the unargued "paradigm" within which its adherents operate. It is to much of contemporary thought what theology was to much of medieval
thought.

It is very instructive to try to sketch how the antirealist approach is manifested in our own society. I will mention a number of areas where one can see its influence. First, we have the
intellectual movements of modernism and postmodernism.
Modernism in philosophy is characterized by antirealism and
skepticism in metaphysics and epistemology, and by relativism
in ethics and politics. Some believe that postmodernism is a new
departure from modernism in that it represents a serious attack

on reason itself. In many ways, it is a radical departure, but one can also make a reasonable case that postmodernism is simply the logical culmination of modernism. Some argue that this is where an attack on realism and truth inevitably ends up—in a nihilistic-type orgy of multiple meanings, clashing viewpoints, contradictory perspectives, *each claiming legitimacy.* Postmodernism may be defined as a critique of objective rationality and identity, and a working out of the implications of this critique for philosophy, literature, and culture. As the postmodernist thinker Jean-François Lyotard notes, postmodernism is "an incredulity towards metanarratives." Postmodernism is, therefore, an attack on reason and on its ability to know reality (and so an attack on philosophy itself). This attack is very broad; it is not an attack on a particular view or a particular philosopher or theory or set of ideas, but an attack on *reason itself*; it is a very sustained attack, and whether one agrees with it or not, it has to be acknowledged that it has been a very influential attack.

Second, we see the attack on reason in the widespread moral relativism of our time. Moral relativism is the view that moral values are relative to either the culture or to the individual. This view is obviously dominant in contemporary culture and usually represents the first line of response in ethical and political debates. As the popular rhetoric goes, "You have your view, and I have my view," which is taken to imply that all views are equally valid. Nobody can impose his or her view on anyone else. Who is to say what is right or wrong? And so on. Of course, there are many well-known contradictions involved in relativism, which stem from the fact that those who employ the language of relativism most loudly and who criticize others for making moral judgments and for trying to impose their morality are usually themselves (1) morally judging others and (2) engaged in the attempt to impose their own moral values on others (and usually on the whole of society)! But such a dominant force has the rhetoric of relativism become in our modern culture that contradicting oneself is no longer something to worry about as long as one's method is politically expedient.

Third, epistemological relativism is rampant today in the universities. Many professors now believe that the pursuit of truth is an old-fashioned idea. This is especially true in the humanit-

ies. One who is unfamiliar with the modern university might be
shocked to hear this, but it is true. And proponents of this view
in the humanities will often use it to attack other disciplines outside the humanities, such as the sciences, claiming perhaps that
our Western approach to science is simply one possible approach among many, which would imply that scientific theories
are not objectively true, but are at best simply cultural perspectives on reality. Other cultures might have (and do have) different approaches to science, and "who is to say" that these are not
legitimate approaches? Once truth is abandoned, all approaches,
no matter how poorly argued for or how poorly supported by
the evidence or how plainly ridiculous, suddenly take on a certain legitimacy.

Fourth, we see this view trickling down to educational theory
and to the whole issue of standards in education. The dummy-
ing down of the curriculum, lamented by so many today in so
many fields, and the corresponding challenge to and rejection of
the traditional curriculum have their origins in the attack on reason that originates in philosophy.

A watchword for many of these contemporary ideas is *tolerance*. And here it is necessary to distinguish between two meanings of the word *tolerance*—the *traditional* meaning and the more
contemporary meaning. *Tolerance* in the traditional sense means
that to be tolerant of something one is willing to consider a view,
to discuss it, to engage in debate with its advocates, but in the
end, one might not accept that the view is true. But one agrees
"to put up with it" to a greater or lesser extent depending on
the issue in question (for example, compare disagreeing with
racism to disagreeing with vegetarianism). This view of tolerance is tied to the notion of truth and would make no sense
without it. For only if you believe in truth, specifically that a
particular view or position is true, can you be tolerant of other
positions with which you disagree. It is only in this sense that
tolerance can be a virtue: it is virtuous to be tolerant of something that you yourself believe to be wrong (depending on the
issue and to what extent, of course). Tolerance is a virtue with a
limit to it, though; if one goes over the limit, one is in the area of
approval, and if one goes too far over the limit, one is in the area
of believing the position oneself! (Compare parents who are

very intolerant of their teenage kids' behavior with parents who are quite strict, with parents who are tolerant, with parents who are excessively tolerant. The first and last groups are off track.)

The more contemporary meaning of tolerance asks one to be tolerant of a view in the sense that one accepts that the view is *philosophically justified*. This is what is meant today when we are asked to be tolerant of abortion, for example. This, of course, is nothing other than a code name for moral relativism—for if one's position is pro-life, then one can be tolerant of abortion only *if one is a moral relativist*. It is not acceptable, according to advocates of the second meaning of tolerance, to be tolerant of something in the sense of just putting up with it, to a greater or lesser extent, even though one disagrees with it. The contemporary meaning of tolerance calls for approval and even endorsement of a view that one believes to be wrong (especially in the area of law). In our society today we are seeing a gradual shift from the traditional meaning of tolerance to the more contemporary meaning. Of course, those who advocate the second meaning of tolerance are not themselves consistent, for they are not really relativists and are quite intolerant of many positions and of the advocates of those positions.

Fifth, another area where we see the attack on reason is in the public versus private distinction, which is very common in the United States. This distinction refers to the issue of holding and living according to one view privately—in one's family, circle of friends, church, etc.—and promoting another view publicly or politically—in civil, legal, and political matters. It is not necessarily that one is happy about maintaining such a distinction, but that one is expected to do so in the modern, liberal, "enlightened" state. This is an important principle of contemporary political liberalism, and I will have more to say about it later. But one of the main reasons why there is pressure on the individual to refrain from bringing one's so-called private beliefs into the public square is that the public square is dominated by relativism. As Justice Anthony Kennedy of the U.S. Supreme Court put it, "At the heart of liberty is the right to define one's own concept of existence, of meaning, of the universe, and of the mystery of human life." Taken to its logical conclusion, Kennedy's position would make the imposition and upholding of law itself impossible.

In contemporary society, all of the above mentioned issues lead to confusion in people's lives because, although I have tried to present them clearly here, in reality these matters are very confusing and interact with each other in a myriad of different ways. Some of these issues might have an influence on a particular person's beliefs more than others; a person might be confused about where she stands on these matters; a person might hold a position that he does not realize has its origins in or that is usually justified by appeal to one or more of the above issues (for example, a person might be anti-abortion, but pro-choice, which is almost always an inconsistent position because the *reason* that one is anti-abortion—that it is the taking of an innocent human life—is strong enough to require one logically to support a legal ban on it). These ideas have made the religious, moral, social, and political landscape so confusing today that people have developed two areas of refuge as a way of coping. These areas of refuge are law and emotion.

When moral relativism becomes dominant, it becomes difficult to adjudicate between moral disputes. When this happens, we fall back on the law and, in particular, on the courts to make our moral decisions for us. However, they do not make these decisions using the language and justification of moral philosophy, for the distinction between morality and law becomes blurred. The moral (and religious) values on which our laws were originally based can now no longer be discussed in any meaningful and productive way, given the widespread moral relativism of our time. This relativistic approach implies in practical terms that there is no objective moral position; that it is just one view pitted against another view in legal terms; that those with the best legal arguments win and so are right. Legal arguments are arguments that appeal to the Constitution, legal precedent, legal loopholes, legal consensus, etc., and, of course, most important of all, to the judge's opinions! This last point is crucial, for it is here that judicial activism has emerged—the tendency of judges not only to interpret the law, but to invent it and to implement their own values through it (the most famous case being *Roe v. Wade*).

Many today lament the way in which judges have begun legislating their own values all over the country, but it is inevitable in a society dominated by moral relativism. For in such a society one simply cannot appeal to reason and truth to settle disputes, so these disputes will end up being settled by whoever has the most power and political will. The law becomes dominant and is used as a political tool in this way, not because people think the society is immoral, but rather because many believe there is no objective morality. (I believe the disputes about genetic engineering, cloning, and so on will be settled in this way in American society—by appeal to the law and to moral relativism. Our society does not have the moral resources to handle these disputes in any other way.)

The other refuge people take in a society dominated by moral relativism is in the realm of emotion. If reason is diminished as a human capacity to seek the truth, to understand the world better, to understand human life better, to help us resolve disputes, to advance our political position or whatever, something must spring forward to fill the vacuum in individuals' lives—and that something is emotion. People begin to look at issues—especially social, religious, moral, political, and legal issues—from an emotional point of view, and they begin to respond to arguments from an emotional standpoint rather than from a rational standpoint. As the philosopher Alasdair MacIntyre has pointed out, today people are far less interested in debating with their opponents and critics; rather, they *protest* against their opponents' positions—an emotional, not a philosophical response. This quickly becomes reified in actual life into the practice that if a person disagrees with my position, he or she is insulting me *personally* rather than respecting me personally and simply disagreeing with my argument. The distinction between a person and his or her argument is lost, and the logical fallacy known as ad hominem (against the man) becomes dominant.

Conversely, one no longer now has to deal with a person's argument; one can simply attack the person, implying (fallaciously) that because the person is morally objectionable, so must be his or her argument. Out of this stance can spring a general practice of labeling positions so as to dismiss them immediately without actually having to debate them. All sides play at this game, including religion. In fact, religions are often quick to attack personally anybody who criticizes religious belief simply because that person has criticized religious belief, rather than looking at the specific arguments of the critique and responding to *them*. But an emotional response is often now the first response to a particular argument rather than a rational one, which is yet another feature of the attack on reason in modern culture.

THE STATE OF RELIGION AT THE MILLENNIUM

Our next concern is inevitably prompted by the points I have already made. Given all of the above, it is appropriate to ask, What is the state of religion at the millennium? In particular, how have the developments discussed above, which are the consequences of the attack on reason and truth, affected the worldview of religion in general? I think that religion is under attack from these developments in a number of ways.

First, religion is obviously under pressure from the claims about the relativity of knowledge and the alleged inability of the human mind to know reality. More particularly, this has the consequence of calling *religious knowledge* into question. Religious worldviews, like all worldviews, make knowledge claims, claims about what really is the case, claims about the nature of God, claims about how we should live our lives, and so on. In fact, it is impossible to hold any worldview and not to make at least some knowledge claims. However, the relativistic attack is used to question the possibility of religious knowledge. Is there such a thing as religious knowledge? Does religion have any truth? Are all religions equally true? Are none true? Is religious morality true? Is religion all just a matter of faith, with no basis in reason or in experience? Is it all just myth and superstition? The attack on knowledge raises these questions. Different religions answer such questions differently; some are inconsistent on these matters, and many are simply confused and are gradually losing their identity.

This is a particularly difficult area for religion because religion has always had as part of its structure a set of metaphysical claims, claims about reality. So if one makes claims about reality, one may be in trouble if an influential movement comes along and asserts that it is not possible to make claims about reality. If one holds, for example, that God exists and has a certain type of nature, these claims are compromised by the attack on knowledge. It is not that the antirealist denies the existence of God; it is a fundamentally deeper issue than this: he or she holds that the truth itself on this or any other issue cannot be known. Now, of course, the antirealist view, in all its various forms, is fraught with inconsistency and contradiction, as I have mentioned (basic material in introductory philosophy courses). But this does not simply mean that as thinkers about these issues we can dismiss such a view and move on with our own beliefs. We cannot do so for two reasons: (1) we are trying to understand the current state of contemporary culture; and (2) these movements, despite their deep problems, have been extremely influential, which in itself is an interesting cultural point. It raises a very interesting question that I will raise but not discuss here: Why has an inconsistent and contradictory attack on reason and truth, the implications of which no one really holds or practices themselves, had such an influence on the modern mind?

Second, religious morality is under attack from moral relativism, which is one of the most obvious effects of the critique of reason on religion today. Religions are now almost actively promoting the idea that one can simply pick and choose one's moral values. They promote this view not in a specific way (yet) but in an abstract way by saying, for example, that one's religion does not promote any particular set of beliefs one has to hold or that the content of one's faith should be determined by other religions or that we should be tolerant (in the *contemporary* sense) of other worldviews, and so on. Now, if one examines these and similar claims carefully, one will see that they make no sense, and that is why *they are stated in the abstract rather than in the concrete* (to state them in the concrete would be to say, for example, that if there is no particular belief one has to hold in a religion, then one could hold a belief totally contrary to the main beliefs of one's religion!). Stating this kind of claim in the abstract obfuscates this inconsistency and also is a good illustration of the influence of relativistic talk on modern religion. The phenomenon of "cafeteria" or "à la carte" religion is an inevitable consequence of this position.

It is interesting to consider for a moment how people make a decision when they are picking from the à la carte religious menu. I do not think their decision is usually based on a philosophical analysis of different positions and on a weighing of the arguments for one over the other. It is usually based on choosing whatever will be expedient in the culture. In this way, people are influenced by secularism and by modernism. And the very phenomenon of an à la carte religion by itself puts further pressure on the truth status of religious belief in general; if one rejects a significant subset of one's religious beliefs but also accepts a significant subset of these beliefs, this fact inevitably by its very nature puts pressure on the half that one accepts, which, whether implicitly or explicitly, could affect one's commitment to these beliefs in one's daily life. Further, the existence of significant numbers of people in this same position further increases the pressure and leads to the phenomenon of religious priests and ministers reluctant to bring up certain topics in their congregations, acting as if such issues are not important or as if they themselves are not committed to them. One might say they do not have the courage of their convictions, but it is more accurate to say that they are playing to an audience who is unsure of theirs and who does not want to be reminded of this fact.

Third, religion is under attack from naturalism, which is the view that all that exists is physical and consequently that there is no God. Naturalism is the modern face of atheism; it is a positive thesis in the sense that it is framed to tell us what a naturalist believes to be true about reality. The naturalist does not defend his view by simply attacking religious belief, which is how atheists traditionally used to defend their view (what I call negative atheism). But if one does not simply attack one's opponent's view, then one needs new, positive arguments to defend one's own view, and here the naturalist usually appeals to science. Naturalism, therefore, promotes the view that religion and science are really opposed and that religion is threatened by science. Naturalists also claim that religion is only myth and superstition, and that science is the only way to knowledge (in this sense, they, too, have been influenced by the attack on reason and take refuge in science). Although I believe it is false that religion is threatened by science and that religion and science are opposed, my point here is that this kind of theme is very dominant in large sections of American society. This view influences ordinary religious people, too, which is why in American society a strict separation of faith and reason has often been promoted, even by religious believers themselves, a point to which I will return later.

Fourth, religion is under attack today from secularism. We can distinguish between philosophical secularism and what we might call, for want of a better term, practical secularism. Philosophical secularism refers to ideologies that are nonreligious—for example, Marxism, secular humanism, naturalism, and so on. These sophisticated theories are advanced as alternatives to religion. If we were to take a head count, we would find that not very many people, as a percentage of the total population, subscribe to these worldviews. Yet secularism is still influential in modern society in a practical sense. Because of practical secularism, religion is being forced more and more out of modern living; there is not as much room for it as there once was in individuals' lives, in part owing to our consumerist society and to the pace of modern life. Even the institutional church has added to this problem. The Roman Catholic Church, for example, abandoned the practice of self-sacrifice on Fridays, moved holy days of obligation to Sundays, and cut back on weekday masses and other services. Perhaps small things in themselves, but their cumulative effect across all religions is deleterious on people's attitudes toward their religious faith. If religious belief is less obvious, it becomes less practiced, less influential, more privatized, and less socially relevant.

Fifth, religion has been adversely affected by the public versus private distinction currently invoked in religious, social, political, and legal debates in our society. The enlightened view is that religion has no place in our political life at all, no place in our public institutions. This argument was recently used with significant effect in the debate in Oregon concerning euthanasia, where the pro-euthanasia side insisted that the arguments against euthanasia were religious arguments, and because religion is a totally private affair, appeal to these arguments is not appropriate when we are dealing with a public issue. This view swayed many people, and the churches were unable to deal with it rhetorically, and so the pro-euthanasia side carried the day. The private/public distinction was used here to put religion on the defensive. Thus, this distinction suits atheists and secular humanists because it enables them to diminish the influence of religion on how people think. The American Civil Liberties Union is a big promoter of this position. It hides behind the founding documents of the United States to defend its approach, but I believe its real motivation is to keep religion on the defensive. But the distinction also suits many religious believers, too, for it gives them a convenient way to support one position privately and another publicly. Abortion is a good example, where a person might be against it privately but support it legally. I believe this interpretation of the U.S. founding documents concerning religion is very erroneous, but I cannot argue that here. But my main point is that as long as this view is the dominant one, it affects religion adversely.

Is Religion Losing Its Influence?

Let us bring our discussion to a conclusion by asking how religion is bearing up under all of these negative influences. Is it strong or weak at the millennium? Another way to consider this issue is to ask: Is religion losing its influence? Of course, these are large and difficult questions, but to give us material for further reflection it is instructive to look at two areas—the institutions of religion and the philosophical and theological state of religion. I will comment briefly on each.

First, I think that, institutionally, religion is weak and floundering, and I mean here religion in general, all religions. One reason for this is that religious leaders and ordinary religious believers are unable to deal with the attacks on religion (described above) in an effective way. The leaders of the institutional church are often rhetorically weak on many contemporary issues and either ignore them altogether or are ineffective in dealing with them. This was obvious in the Oregon case. Religious leaders in Oregon were reluctant to advance the position that an argument against euthanasia does not necessarily have to be religious in a narrow sectarian sense, that one can give a perfectly respectable philosophical argument against euthanasia. This argument is based on the *principle* that human life is sacred, is of supreme value, is the most cherished value in human existence, and so on, and that the introduction of euthanasia would compromise and cheapen the value of life. It is important to note that this argument is not essentially a *Catholic* or a *religious* argument in a sectarian sense because it makes no specific appeal to religious beliefs or principles in its general outline and because it is an argument that is accepted by many atheists and secular humanists. The second line of argument against euthanasia is what I call the "practical argument." This argument is founded on the *practical abuses* that would inevitably result if euthanasia were to be introduced. It relies on the general point that euthanasia is impractical because it could not be adequately regulated through legislation. Churches have mainly concentrated on the "practical" argument and have downplayed the "in principle" argument. And so they backed off in Oregon and lost, which is partly a failure of leadership.

This kind of approach leads to further problems because then the churches' views are not heard; it is one thing for one's view to be heard and rejected, but it is quite another for one's view not to be a player at all in the debate. Poor leadership in the churches unwittingly helps the enemies of religion, and there are many groups waiting to take political advantage. The churches also are not as countercultural as they might be; they often seem to be mirroring the culture rather than subjecting it to critical examination. My view is that religious leaders could make a real impression on the political debates of the day and could inform these debates in an insightful and morally worthwhile way—in a way that many people would appreciate and welcome—but they have failed in this task.

Second, from the philosophical point of view, I believe that Christianity (which is the only religion I feel competent to discuss here) and Catholicism in particular have great strengths. Catholicism has always been a great defender of reason in religious belief—of the attempt to show that belief in God is a rational belief and that religious belief is more rational than any atheistic alternative. In his recent encyclical *Fides et Ratio* (Faith and Reason), Pope John Paul II made a very interesting point when he noted that it is ironic that at this stage in our history it is the Church that is among the foremost defenders of reason and truth, of the objectivity of knowledge, of common sense, whereas many times throughout history those who have claimed to defend reason and truth have often ridiculed the Church for being on the side of superstition and myth. The Catholic Church, in particular, has always insisted on a significant role for reason in religious belief and in theology. It has always defended the view that faith and reason are compatible—that the truths of faith are not incompatible with the truths of reason and, more significantly, that religious faith is a rational response to the ultimate mystery of the universe and of human life. The Catholic Church has great resources to defend its worldview and its philosophy of the human person in the light of secular opposition and attack. This is one of the reasons the Catholic Church is much disliked by many intellectuals: it represents a serious and rational alternative to their worldview and hence is a threat to that view.

Catholicism differs from various forms of Protestantism on the question of faith and reason. The Protestant tradition in the United States has mostly stressed the difference between faith and reason, and has promoted the view that reason and faith are two separate and mutually exclusive domains of knowledge. This approach has had the advantage of protecting faith from criticism because it avoids rational analysis and debate; the disadvantage is that one's religion progressively over time becomes marginalized. People begin to regard it as being outside the mainstream of reason, belonging to a purely private realm, where it should not have any influence on public affairs. This practice feeds, first, the private/public distinction and, second, the view that all religions can be lumped together in a private realm. The intelligentsia's reaction to the Heaven's Gate cult suicide a few years back brought out this second point clearly— they were very reluctant to criticize this cult, even though they believed the actions of its members were morally evil. Their reaction was based on the notion that because the actions of the cult members were religiously motivated, they were not subject to rational analysis. But in simply regarding this cult as just another religion, they promote the view that one can make no distinction between rational and irrational religions. But once one insists on such a distinction, then the public/private distinction must be greatly modified, and one can make a case for introducing rational religious arguments into the public square. From the secular point of view, there is an advantage to lumping all religions together: one can keep them in a private realm where they cannot have much influence.

Many religions, but Catholicism in particular, provide a strong critique of naturalism. This is because the philosophy of the human person, subscribed to by many religions, is supported by a strong rational defense and is appealing to many people. Simply put, this is the view that human beings are rational animals, made of body and soul, who have free will and who seek happiness, which is bound up with love and with living a moral life and ultimately with God. The naturalists get into difficulties with their view of the human person, and I will mention here just one area that gives them special trouble—free will. Many naturalists do not believe in free will because they cannot reconcile it with their account of reality, which attempts to explain everything purely in terms of the laws of physics. If everything that exists is physical and follows the laws of science, then the mind is just the brain, and so human actions are all causally determined—and so, however unpalatable it may be, there is no free will. This is a very odd view to hold, for it would mean that morality, politics, punishment, and responsibility would all be compromised; yet it is a consequence of naturalism. And it is incredibly counterintuitive.

Another problem for naturalism is that it denies a cause to and an ultimate purpose for the universe. Religion, on the other hand, defends design and purpose in human life; secular views cannot do this, for if one believes that the universe and human life are the products of chance, then it is very difficult to believe that there is an overall purpose to life. This presents the naturalist and the secular humanist with a philosophical problem, which for many in the twentieth century has led to practical problems in daily living and has presaged the nihilistic air of much of modern life, as expressed in many works of art and literature. This does not mean that one can just turn around and say that God must exist, and then the philosophical and practical problems disappear. What the Roman Catholic Church advocates is that the argument that God exists is a rational argument, and if one wants to consider the cumulative case for each view side by side, then religion is more rational than any atheistic alternative.

Religion also offers a strong critique of secularism and of the excesses of capitalism (one of the themes of the article by Gerald Miller in chapter 7 of this volume). I cannot go into this point here at any length, but the themes Miller develops, with which I thoroughly agree, flow out of the Christian view of the human person. The Christian philosophy of the person stresses inter-subjectivity—the social nature of the person, where the person is social by nature and not just by choice. This means that self-interest is not our main motivation in our moral and social relations with others. This view is critical of the dominant view today in political theory that holds that we are all autonomous individuals, little centers of rational decision making, and that we enter society by choice and not by nature. Service to others flows out of the Christian view of the person. This is a very profound view, far superior in my view to any secular alternative. It has been excellently laid out by Pope John Paul II in a variety of encyclicals throughout his pontificate. Indeed, the pope's speech to the United Nations in 1995 was an inspiring statement of the Christian view of the human person and how it functions as a necessary corrective to the excesses of capitalism, naturalism, and the utilitarian and self-centered philosophies of the modern era.

To conclude, then, I believe that religion is under attack, but that it has the resources to deal with its critics. I think it is the most reasonable worldview and that it can be defended philosophically. Philosophers who are religious believers can help in that defense. It is difficult to predict the future of religion, but I do think that it has been weakened by these modern trends and that the trend is still in the direction of weakening it further. We have yet to see on a broad level a competent, strong, and sustained defense of religion in contemporary American society.

Bibliography

Audi, R., and N. Wolterstorff. *Religion in the Public Square*. Lanham, Md.: Rowman and Littlefield, 1997.

Jaki, Stanley. *Cosmos and Creator*. Edinburgh: Scottish Academic, 1980.

John Paul II. "Address to the United Nations." October 5, 1995. Available at www.vatican.va.

———. *Evangelium Vitae* (The Gospel of Life). March 25, 1995.

———. *Fides et Ratio* (Faith and Reason). September 14, 1998.

———. *Laborem Exercens* (On Human Work). September 14, 1981.

———. *Veritatis Splendor* (The Splendor of Truth). August 6, 1993.

MacIntyre, Alasdair. *After Virtue*. 2d ed. Notre Dame: University of Notre Dame Press, 1984.

Mackie, J. L. *The Miracle of Theism*. Oxford: Oxford University Press, 1982.

Sandel, Michael, ed. *Liberalism and Its Critics*. New York: New York University Press, 1984.

Sweetman, Brendan, ed. *The Failure of Modernism*. Washington, D.C.: AMA, Catholic University of America Press, 1999.

———. "Postmodernism, Derrida, and *Différance:* A Critique." *International Philosophical Quarterly* 39, no. 1 (March 1999): 5–18.

Sweetman, Brendan, and Curtis Hancock. *Truth and Religious Belief*. Armonk, N.Y.: M. E. Sharpe, 1998.

Swinburne, Richard. *The Existence of God*. Rev. ed. Oxford: Oxford University Press, 1991.

3

The Perennial Philosophy: A Tonic for What Ails Us

Curtis L. Hancock

THIS IS AN ESSAY on education. Even though the word *education* does not appear in the title, that is nonetheless what my discussion is about in essence. In this chapter, I refer to a philosophical tradition that I think can supply the best foundation for education. It is for this reason that I am interested in this tradition. I am not interested in it for nostalgic or antiquarian reasons. It has my attention because I think that it makes sense and that it is timely. It is sensible because it rests on a highly effective account of knowledge and on a convincing philosophy of the human person. With these correct foundations, this tradition can educate the whole person: intellect, will, and spiritual development. By its account of knowledge, it can explain our intellect. Furthermore, because its view of knowledge is very comprehensive, it can explain moral knowledge, thus educating our will. It can help us make reasonable judgments about good or evil, right or wrong, justice or injustice. Additionally, by being open to the question of God and the significance of that question in human life, it can address issues involving our spiritual development. This tradition provides a holistic view of education, which makes it very timely. It helps us overcome some of the arbitrary limitations about knowledge and the human person common in education today. This tradition, then, is, in a manner of speaking, a tonic for what ails us.

This philosophical tradition is a wisdom that the Catholic faith has uniquely developed and bequeathed to posterity. It has been called by some of its defenders, such as Jacques Maritain, the "perennial philosophy" (from the Latin, *philosophia perennis*).

In a nutshell (at the price of oversimplification), the perennial philosophy is the philosophy of the ancient Greeks absorbed into the Christian wisdom of the Roman Catholic Church. The Church saw in the philosophy of the ancient Greeks two very important things: an account of knowledge that could be in service for Christian wisdom and also a philosophy of the human person that could support and complement the Christian vision of moral life and human destiny. The perennial philosophy refers to the way the Catholic Church Christianized or "baptized" Greek philosophy. But the absorption of classical wisdom does not stop there. The perennial philosophy ultimately refers to the way the Church assimilated the Greek wisdom into a synthesis of philosophical and theological understanding that borrowed from multiple ancient and medieval cultures, including Jewish, Islamic, and Roman philosophy.

One can, no doubt, infer here an important conclusion. Because the Church has sought assistance from philosophical traditions, it has had historically a very favorable attitude about the relationship of reason to faith. Reason can assist the Church in its exploration and defense of the faith, a project St. Augustine called *fides quaerens intellectum:* faith seeking understanding. The view that the relationship between faith and reason can be constructive has been the hallmark of Catholic education. Certainly, it has been championed by the doctors of the Church.

I think that this synthetic philosophy has a special power. In fact, it has shaped the Western world, if the truth be known. If we retain our memory of it and if we continue to apply it to modern life, it can help us correct many of the intellectual and moral difficulties that beset us. Before I comment further on the nature of the perennial philosophy, its special power, and its useful applications to today's educational needs, I would like to recall how I came to appreciate it.

A REMINISCENCE

I did something unusual as I graduated from high school. I declared philosophy as my major even before I entered the University of Oklahoma in 1968. This is not to suggest that I was especially academic. In fact, my main interest in college was athletics. I told my parents that I was going to college to be a runner. I attended OU on a cross-country and track scholarship. Running is really all I cared about at that time of my life. (My wife might tell you that it seems to be all I care about now, but that's another story.) Nonetheless, I had done some reading on my own, especially science fiction and even some Thoreau and Emerson. These writers spoke of things "philosophical." Philosophy seemed to involve interesting and deep subjects, so I thought I would enjoy reading more philosophy. I declared philosophy my major, with no more thought to it than that.

My parents, neither of whom had a college degree (although my father had picked up some hours on the GI Bill), sensed that the university might affect me in ways over and beyond athletics—that it would engage me intellectually. But in spite of this overall favorable attitude, my mother nevertheless expressed some alarm when I told her that I was going to major in philosophy. She believed—and I discovered later that her belief was not entirely without foundation—that the study of philosophy at today's secular universities is sometimes an attempt at apostasy. Unfortunately, there are some professors who believe that the essence of philosophical pedagogy is to take "naive," "superstitious" young minds and turn them into "enlightened" atheists. But I assured her that my faith would not be rattled at school, and I left it at that.

Of course, within months of studying philosophy at the university, I had become an atheist and had become convinced that people needed religion as a crutch, just as the distinguished governor of Minnesota now believes. Religious people were superstitious and believed in unprogressive things, ill-suited for a scientific age. I frequently made it a point to carry A. J. Ayer's *Language, Truth, and Logic* and Bertrand Russell's *Why I Am Not a Christian* on my walks and visits, pulling out their words whenever the occasion called for them. I and a few of my unbelieving friends used to pester especially members of the Fellowship of Christian Athletes who lived with us in the athletic dorm. One of the members gave me a copy of C. S. Lewis's *Mere Christianity*. For eighteen years that book sat on my shelf. By the time I got around to reading it, I had come on my own to accept almost everything in it. I wish I had read it earlier. It might have cut short that long eighteen-year pilgrimage. I make it a practice of reading that book once a year, usually on a hiking trip I take out west somewhere. I've read it approximately twelve times, as a result.

Because I declared philosophy my major as an incoming freshman, I was able to accumulate in four years a good number of philosophy credits: forty-six hours, to be exact. Many of those courses were taught by professors who dismissed the idea of Christian wisdom as oxymoronic or, more probably, as just plain moronic. But by my senior year, my reading had brought me to a new openness about religion. I began to experience something Francis Bacon once said: "a little or superficial knowledge of philosophy may incline the mind of man to atheism, but a further proceeding therein doth bring the mind back again to religion" (4). I found that to be the case in my own life and in the lives of several other philosophers whom I have known. Those philosophers are persons whose lives I have found to be morally integrated, personally strengthened, and interpersonally enriched by their philosophical study, and their examples have helped persuade me of the importance and power of a philosophical formation that involves theism.

The good fortune of encountering a brilliant teacher assisted me greatly in the evolution of which Bacon spoke. Near the end of my undergraduate experience, I matriculated into the courses of Francis Kovach, a proud Hungarian, whose zealous allegiance to his homeland was rivaled only by his devotion to the writings of St. Thomas Aquinas. Kovach introduced me to ancient and medieval philosophy, the wellsprings of the perennial philosophy, especially manifest in the writings of Aristotle and Aquinas. Upon studying these thinkers, I realized that there were other ways of looking at the deeper issues of life. I began to suspect that my skeptical professors were neglecting to tell me about views different from their own in the history of philosophy. As I explored that history more and more, I encountered the perennial philosophy, which was quite liberating because I discovered its countercultural power and its ability to address more effectively the classical problems of the human condition— God, knowledge, morality, and politics.

After many years of exploring the perennial philosophy, I decided to devote my life as an educator to assist in keeping its voice alive in the intellectual culture—which is not an easy task in today's skeptical, relativist climate and postmodernist malaise. In fact, some declare that the perennial philosophy is dead, which would be an ironic condition for a philosophy that's supposed to be perennial. But rumors of its death, I suspect, have been greatly exaggerated. Like others before me, I predict that it will survive to bury its undertakers.

The Perennial Philosophy

In the remainder of my discussion, I specify further the perennial philosophy by examining the expression itself, analyzing the terms *philosophy* and *perennial*. Additionally, I make a few observations about the historical genesis of this philosophy. Finally, I discuss how it can help us put education on firmer ground by showing how it can assess certain common assumptions about knowledge. If these assumptions are left unaddressed, they seriously impede the task of education, especially if we aspire to educate the whole person: intellect, will, and spiritual development.

I stated earlier that the Roman Catholic Church acquired its view of philosophy primarily from the ancient Greeks. It is natural, then, to remind ourselves of what the Greeks meant by the term *philosophy*. In ancient Greek, as we all know, *philosophy* means love of wisdom. According to the Greeks, wisdom is the highest kind of knowledge. It is not just knowledge; it is a very special kind of knowledge. It is more than just an accumulation of facts or raw data. It takes what one already knows and attempts to give it a deeper explanation and justification. It gives this deeper justification by helping one discover the causes of things. That is how the Greeks liked to put it. "Philosophy is a search for the ultimate causes of things." Philosophy, then, does not teach new information; it deepens, refines, and develops what we already know, our common awarenesses.

If wisdom is an exploration of what we already know, then all of us are already philosophers. As a result, philosophy is everybody's business. If philosophy examines what is given to us in common experience, then the subject matter of philosophy is available to everybody. This attitude about philosophy goes by the name *commonsense "realism."*

Now, though you might think that this philosophical attitude of the ancient Greek realists was uneventful, in fact it was really earth shaking and revolutionary. Why? Religious authorities in ancient times disliked and suspected philosophy, because there is something democratic about philosophy if it is accessible to everybody and if it is everybody's business. The ancient Greek religion taught that there was a privileged class of poets and religious authorities who knew things quite inaccessible to the ordinary person. There was an explicit elitism in the religion. The religious expert knew because he or she was in the gods' favor. "Zeus likes me more than he does you" expressed the mythopoet's conception of wisdom. The philosophers over-turned this idea. Thinkers such as Socrates and Anaxagoras championed the ordinary person's ability to think about matters clearly and effectively so as to acquire wisdom without divine inspiration. Accordingly, philosophy seriously threatened the religious authorities. Not surprisingly, philosophers were some-times persecuted and killed in ancient Greece. Anaxagoras and Socrates are cases in point. From their examples, we still remem-ber and appreciate that one of the virtues of a philosophical edu-cation is its countercultural power. (Modern philosophy, by the way, tragically and mistakenly reversed this relationship and turned philosophy into something elitist, but that's a story for another day.)

This view of philosophy as based on a reflection of common experience is clearly reflected in the interests of the early Greek thinkers—for example, matter, change, causality, and the prob-lem of the one and the many. The principle of "being" also occu-pied their interest. Although such a principle sounds forbidding, it too obviously arises out of ordinary experience. Acquaintance with *things that are* is self-evident. But just what does it mean *to be?* The Greeks asked this question and gave birth to metaphys-ics. Still, no matter how sophisticated their reflections became on the subject, they understood and appreciated that the question emerges out of ordinary experience. (Bill Clinton notwithstand-

ing, the word *is* has a sense and a usage that most people basically grasp. Although Clinton's utterances on the subject sound
Eleatic, Parmenides was a better guide than the president in un-
packing the term.)

The Greeks also discussed just who is this being, this human
person, for whom such things are an issue. They asked, What is
it to be a human person? And how should the human person
live his or her life so as to attain happiness for the individual
and the community?

By the time Greek philosophy matured—for example, in the
works of Plato and Aristotle and later in thinkers such as Ploti-
nus—there emerged a strong belief that a powerful reflection on
our ordinary experience can give us significant indications about
things that lie even outside ordinary experience. In other words,
they became convinced that philosophical reasoning, starting as
it does in natural experience, can justify belief in things outside
natural experience, that philosophy can entertain and respond
intelligently to the three great questions: God, freedom, and immortality.

These last remarks are very important because they show that
even in an ancient, non-Christian, intellectual milieu these issues
were not regarded as mere superstitions. Even before the era of
Christian belief, pagan thinkers defended these beliefs as rational and in many cases went so far as to declare them as truths
accessible to human understanding and demonstration. This
point should be kept in mind when critics of Christianity say
that such beliefs have no relation to reason and thus are superstitions.

The question must be asked, "How does Catholicism fit into
this picture?" The answer lies in the fact that the early Church
Fathers and later most of the great thinkers in the Middle Ages
discovered in this classical Greek and Hellenistic wisdom an in-
valuable resource as the Roman Catholic Church sought to advance its knowledge of the articles of faith; philosophy gave
theologians principles, distinctions, and terms so as to explicate
Scripture and Church teaching. The Church also found in philosophy a way to defend the faith against those who would dismiss it as mere superstition. The classic religious beliefs—God,
freedom, and immortality—could also be given a rational de-

fense, at least to a modest *but significant* degree. Ironically, the Catholic religion did something the ancient Greek religion did not do. It accepted philosophical reason and accommodated it to its own methods and theological wisdom. In this way, philosophy found a religious patron and home, and became *Christian philosophy*.

I do not mean to suggest that somehow philosophy is able to rationalize every article of faith or that somehow reason eliminates mystery from faith. Far from it. But reason has a relation to faith and can come to its assistance, as far as reason is able given its own limited and humble powers.

Pope John Paul II expressed this vision of philosophy in his recent encyclical, *Fides et Ratio*. The following quotation captures the spirit of what I have said thus far:

> Although times change and knowledge increases, it is possible to discern a core of philosophical insight within the history of thought as a whole. Consider, for example, the principles of non-contradiction, finality and causality, as well as the concept of the person as a free and intelligent subject with the capacity to know God, truth and goodness. Consider as well certain fundamental moral norms which are shared by all. These are among the indications that beyond different schools of thought there exists a body of knowledge which may be judged a kind of spiritual heritage of humanity. It is as if we had come upon an implicit philosophy, as a result of which all feel that they possess these principles, albeit in a general and unreflective way. Precisely because it is shared in some measure by all, this knowledge should serve as a kind of reference point for the different philosophical schools.
>
> . . .
>
> On her part, the Church cannot but set great value upon reason's drive to attain goals which render people's lives ever more worthy. She sees in philosophy the way to come to know fundamental truths about human life. At the same time, the Church considers philosophy an indispensable help for a deeper understanding of faith and for communicating the truth of the Gospel to those who do not yet know it. (4–5)

It is noteworthy that the Holy Father says that this implicit philosophy "is shared in some measure by all." Such a remark indicates why this Catholic intellectual tradition is called not just a "philosophy," but a "perennial philosophy." The word *perennial* means enduring, constant, forever vital and applicable. Accordingly, the perennial philosophy can endure across the ages. Because it is built on principles that originate in the common experience of all human beings, its principles can speak to all human beings, across historical and cultural boundaries. Its principles, then, never go out of style because they must be always involved, at least *implicitly* as John Paul II puts it, in any generation's effort to understand reality and the human condition. As a result, the perennial philosophy can speak to us today just as effectively as it did, say, to Aristotle in the fourth century B.C.

Thomas Aquinas, who is this tradition's greatest representative, explains theologically that the perennial philosophy is common and implicit to all cultures and to every generation. He reasoned that because God is the truth and the author of all truth, no truth can offend God. Hence, no matter what its historical, cultural, or even religious origin, every truth is "God friendly," if you will. So Christianity must be open to all truth or knowledge regardless of who discovers it or where. For this reason, contrary to what you sometimes hear from its critics, Christianity is, *in principle*, an *inclusivist* tradition.

In fact, its inclusivism caused difficulties for St. Thomas Aquinas, who saw the perennial philosophy as a multicultural achievement. Many of his contemporaries did not appreciate this view. They could not see how a Christian philosopher could accommodate contributions from Islamic, Jewish, or even pagan cultures. At any rate, Aquinas's effort to synthesize these schools and influences caused quite a stir. His effort was quite revolutionary. Authorities usually suspect revolutionaries. Not surprisingly, the bishop of Paris condemned Aquinas's writings in 1277, three years after his death.

A Tonic for What Ails Us

It seems to me that we need St. Thomas's "revolting" philosophy now more than ever. It is a tonic for what ails us. Why do I say that? Because it has, as I indicated before, a confidence in the power of reason, given its proper limits, to engage in a dialogue with modern assumptions about knowledge and to test them for their adequacy. In this examination, the perennial philosophy can show that many common assumptions about knowledge today arbitrarily limit and undermine the task of education.

What are these assumptions about knowledge? Space permits me to list and evaluate only three of them. Certainly, more than these three can be enumerated, but for the sake of brevity I have decided to focus only on them.

   a. Knowledge is, in the last analysis, merely a paradigm, a
      theoretical perspective constructed by culture, language,
      or our own psychology, and therefore does not tell us
      what the world really is.
   b. Empirical science and mathematics are the only genuine
      ways of knowing.
   c. Faith is altogether separate from reason, so much so that
      reason is irrelevant to matters of faith.

Now, let me comment briefly on each of them, showing thereby how the perennial philosophy can recommend an alternative, more plausible way to think about knowledge.

a. *Knowledge is, in the last analysis, merely a paradigm, a theoretical perspective constructed by culture, language, or our own psychology and therefore does not tell us what the world really is.*

This assumption derives from a very basic fallacy, an error in reasoning. It results from taking a trivial fact—that we always bring something of ourselves and our own upbringing, experience, and cultural background to our knowledge—and using it to draw a radical conclusion, that knowledge is ultimately some kind of cultural construction. This move is, of course, quite invalid. Culture may influence what we know, but it need not construct or invent what we know. We may grant that culture, personality, temperament, experience, and language influence our knowledge, but that does not necessitate the conclusion that knowledge cannot tell us about the world outside ourselves or outside our culture. A more balanced position—that in spite of our personal and cultural influences, we might still know objective and real things—is bypassed for the extreme view that knowledge is just a construction, ultimately just a reflection of some social or personal prejudice.

Let me offer an illustration of how this fashionable belief appears in academic culture today. Last year I taught a class in Aristotle. One day while browsing at a bookstore, I discovered a little book on Aristotle by a scholar named Paul Strathern: *Aristotle in 90 Minutes*. I read the book in one sitting, although I probably took more than the obligatory ninety minutes; I have been told that I move my lips when I read.

After his mixed effort at summarizing Aristotle's philosophy, Strathern closes the book by passing judgment on the ancient Stagirite. The problem with Aristotle, Strathern says, is that he thought that the mind could know the truth. Aristotle failed to grasp "that there can be no such a thing as a 'true' way of viewing the world, either scientifically or philosophically. The conclusions we reach simply depend on the paradigms we adopt: the way we decide to think about the world. In other words, there is no such thing as ultimate truth" (55).

There are so many things objectionable in this statement that I could amplify this chapter into a book, but let me just focus on its most obvious failing: it contradicts itself. If one's knowledge is bound within a paradigm, how can one transcend this paradigm in order to judge fairly that another paradigm is wrong? To do so is to achieve precisely the kind of transcendent perspective on things that Strathern says one cannot achieve. How can one compare one paradigm as better or worse if one cannot step outside them? Aristotle, he says, is wrong because Aristotle believes that we can get outside our paradigms (so as to make justifiable claims about what the world is), and yet Strathern steps outside his own paradigm to condemn Aristotle. So why isn't Strathern wrong? This is an egregious inconsistency.

In my experience, I have found that those who preach paradigms are willing quite often to do what they say one cannot do: step outside one's paradigm and judge other positions as inferior. If they were consistent, they would say, "I have my paradigm (or prejudice), and you have yours." But such a statement would be very uninteresting and make their position trivial. It would mean that they could not criticize other points of view that they do not like. So, more often than not they preach that those who disagree with them cannot judge them because every-thing is a paradigm, whereas somehow they themselves are nonetheless privileged to judge their opponents' paradigms as unworthy. They usually take the position that Strathern does: judging that their paradigm is more enlightened than paradigms or philosophies of the past, especially more advanced than those such as Aristotle's, which deny in the first place that we are im-prisoned in our paradigms.

Many people today ignore these logical problems because if they talk like Strathern—if they say, "the conclusions we reach simply depend on the paradigms we adopt"—it makes them sound tolerant, multicultural, and progressive. It makes philoso-phy sound as if it is just a matter of choice, and *choice* is a rhetori-cally powerful and persuasive word in our culture today. But, in reality, Strathern's view makes none of these values really possi-ble because it collapses into moral relativism, the belief that there is no objective right or wrong. This conclusion follows from his view because if there is no way to justify truth objec-tively, there is no way to justify the truth of moral claims objec-tively. If ethics, like every other idea, is just a perspective, a paradigm, an intellectual or cultural construction, how can one justify the values of tolerance or multiculturalism or progress?

Why is tolerance better than intolerance if value is just an in-vention, just another arbitrary option among a cafeteria line of alternatives? If you cannot judge another culture, how can you judge its members wrong if they choose to be intolerant?

Likewise, such relativism would make multiculturalism im-possible. If you believe in objective values, you can believe in multiculturalism because you can make the case that in other societies there are *really* things worthwhile. But if you are a rela-tivist, you do not believe that things are ever *really* worthwhile. The most you can say is that some people happen to *feel* that certain things are worthwhile. So on what basis do you advocate multiculturalism? On its own terms, relativism would furnish just as much a warrant for monoculturalism as it would multi-culturalism. If it advocates the latter, it is just imposing its view on others arbitrarily. But isn't it the relativist who says "you must never impose your views or pass judgment"?

Relativism also rules out the idea of progress. To compare a progressive culture with an unprogressive culture requires a norm above them both. But according to the relativist, there is no such norm outside the paradigms! If a culture overcomes the enslavement of individuals, the subjugation of women, the oppression of children and of minorities, how can you praise them if there are no defensible moral standards to do so?

So relativism is a siren song. Homer told us that sailors often crashed their ships into the rocks, mesmerized by the inviting but in the end destructive song of the sirens. Relativism functions analogously in our society today, deceiving us into thinking that it can do certain things for us when it cannot.

This point must not be lost on us; otherwise, one risks falling into the awkward and comic situation that the valedictorian of a distinguished university found herself in a few years ago. Having ingested this relativism about truth, she boasted that she was grateful that no professor ever had the gall during her four years of college education to tell her anything was really true. Of course, she spoke these words standing behind a lectern with the seal of the university embossed on it, with the Latin word *Veritas* boldly evident. I wonder if, when her parents heard her remarks, they realized that her tuition had not been a prudent expenditure, for if there is no knowledge, there is no education, and *truth* is another word for knowledge. That is what the word *education* signifies. It comes from the Latin *exducere,* to lead out of, to lead out of ignorance into knowledge or truth. So her parents (or someone else or some institution) paid handsome money for an education when none was presumably acquired, according to their daughter's own words. But bemusedly we observe that she was disingenuous, of course. She neglected to note that some educator obviously told her that relativism was true!

b. *Empirical science and mathematics are the only genuine ways of knowing.*

A number of remarks are called for here. Obviously, this proposition is self-refuting because it itself is neither a scientific nor a mathematical remark. The truth of this proposition is established neither by scientific method nor by mathematical demonstrations.

Second, the claim that science is the only way of knowing seems counterintuitive. Science can, for example, tell you how to clone somebody, but it cannot tell you whether or not you should. Science can *describe* how to make a plutonium bomb, but it cannot *prescribe* whether or not you use it. In other words, there seems to be an area of knowledge called "moral under-standing" that is outside the reach of science. It is not science; nonetheless, it makes claims that are defensible.

Third, one way to assess the adequacy of a theory is to draw out its logical consequences. If they seem incredible, they cast doubt on the soundness of the theory. What follows from the belief that because knowledge must have measurable objects, ethical judgments become mere matters of taste? It leads to the incredible conclusion that every conceivable variety of moral outrage and crime, from slavery and racism to murder and infanticide, is just a matter of taste. Because the Holocaust is not measurable, because the sins of Auschwitz are not six meters high and weigh two tons, their evil is not really knowable. Somehow they are just a feeling, a taste, an opinion, a prejudice. I myself am not willing to reduce our moral convictions to mere taste just because someone has a narrow, self-refuting theory of knowledge.

Some thinkers go the full nine yards and even declare that only physically measurable things can even exist. This belief is called *naturalism* and by its critics *dogmatic materialism*. Common spokespersons for this view are Carl Sagan, Richard Dawkins, Stephen Jay Gould, and Stephen Hawking, who in his book *A Brief History of Time* "proceeds on the assumption that what is not measurable by physicists does not have any existence in reality," as Mortimer Adler sums it up (*Intellect* 107).

That this belief is quite arbitrary and unconvincing can be made evident very simply. When a naturalist, such as Hawking, utters his judgment that only matter exists, he states his belief with the assumption that it has meaning. He means what he says. He knows it with his mind, and he assumes that you who hear or read the proposition likewise have minds. But a mind is not something that can be measured by the physical sciences. Minds are not physical things. Neurology could develop a complete map of your brain, but that would not necessarily show what your thoughts are. A scientist who was deaf from birth could exhaustively describe all the physical mechanisms involved in hearing, but that still could not tell her what it is to hear. Consciousness and experience, the contents of mind, are not the same as the nervous system, however much they may be associated with it. So by using his mind, Hawking refutes his own belief in naturalism!

c. *Faith is altogether separate from reason, so much so that reason is irrelevant to matters of faith.*

The perennial philosophy protests against this view by arguing the following: faith may transcend reason, but it does not invalidate reason, nor does it render reason irrelevant to the life of the believer or to the contents of religious faith. Faith may contain many elements of the nonrational, but it is not irrational. In fact, as I said earlier, philosophical reason can examine and defend three of the great religious beliefs—God, freedom, and immortality.

As I make this point, I recall Edmund Burke's statement that "superstition is the religion of the feebleminded." This claim may sound like what the governor of Minnesota thinks about religion, but in reality Burke's remark is quite different. Jesse the Mind thinks that religion is the superstition of the feebleminded, whereas Burke is careful to say that superstition is the religion of the feebleminded. Religion need not be superstitious, even though sadly many people take their superstitions and virtually turn them into a religion.

So the perennial philosophy argues for a more balanced and reasonable consideration of the relationship between faith and reason. It argues that faith should not be put in some hermetically sealed private sphere that is irrelevant to the life of the mind in philosophy, say, or science or politics. Religion can speak to these issues, too, and should have a peer voice in the public square, so that its point of view can help advance such debates. If religion can be rational, even if not fully demonstrable, it can be defended by reason, and when philosophical, scientific, moral, or political claims contradict it, it can dispute them in the public square.

For example, if a scientist says that certain races are inferior, as Darwin did in *The Descent of Man* and as Shockley did more recently, or that human beings are not free, as B. F. Skinner believed, the religious thinker can employ science and philosophy to show that these views, which quite evidently contradict Christian faith, can be demonstrated on rational grounds to be wrong. In this way, reason is relevant to faith and can directly and indirectly support its credibility. Reason can help us understand the content of faith better and can even assist us in defending faith against those who would attack it as mere superstition.

In my opinion, if educated Christians do not appreciate and judiciously employ the power of reason in their presentation and defense of the Christian worldview, we, as a Christian culture, are going to become increasingly marginalized in the intellectual and political debate. By default, our interests will be ignored in the wider society. We will become the intellectual equivalents of the Amish community, seen as an eccentricity, perhaps even patronized in a way, but altogether marginalized and ineffectual in advancing Christian wisdom and values.

CONCLUSION

We can prevent that marginalization from happening if we retain and use the perennial philosophy to keep Christian education strong and to equip future generations with the intellectual resources to defend Christian values in the public square. This effort can be persuasive because it is based on the unity and the inclusiveness of truth. Just as the perennial philosophy enabled the Roman Catholic Church to synthesize the principles and values of multiple civilizations in the first and second millennia, it can analogously adapt to the third millennium. In this way, it can serve a powerful constructive purpose as it helps humankind maintain its balance by absorbing what is best in modern pluralism while avoiding its disorienting elements. It can provide a meeting place for all humanity as we develop a discourse scaffolded on the implicit philosophy. It provides a block in a foundation *ut unum sint:* so that all may be one.

WORKS CITED

Adler, Mortimer. *Aristotle for Everybody.* New York: Macmillan, 1978.

————. *Intellect: Mind over Matter.* New York: Macmillan, 1990.

Ayer, A. J. *Language, Truth, and Logic.* New York: Dover, 1952.

Bacon, Francis. *The Advancement of Learning.* Vol. 30 of *Great Books of the Western World,* edited by Robert Maynard Hutchins. Chicago: Encyclopedia Britannica, 1952.

Hawking, Stephen. *A Brief History of Time.* New York: Bantam, 1978.

John Paul II. *Fides et Ratio.* September 14, 1998.

Russell, Bertrand. *Why I Am Not a Christian.* New York: Allen and Unwin, 1957.

Strathern, Paul. *Aristotle in 90 Minutes.* Chicago: Ivan R. Dee, 1996.

4

"In the Beginning Was the Word": The Word, Truth, and Catholicism at the Millennium

Joseph A. Cirincione

THE GOSPEL according to John opens metaphorically with lines of poetry that express multiple meanings. In technical terms, the language employs a *tenor* ("the subject of the comparison, what is to be compared") and several *vehicles* ("what the subject is compared to or with" [Barton and Hudson 99]) to express John's vision. The Catholic Church and other Christian believers and theologians have for centuries assumed that they have progressively explicated the truth of John's metaphors. Recent epistemological claims, however, have called their assumption into question.

John's opening lines try to get at the essence of "the Word" by metaphorically likening it to an entity that both "was with God" and "was God"—a puzzle to be sure. Further, because "All things came to be through him," the Word was also somehow the source of all creation. It is possible that the Word was Creator or that the Creator somehow worked through the Word. Similarly, "What came to be through him was life," suggesting either that the Word created life or was instrumental in making life a reality.

That "this life was the light of the human race" adds to the vehicles that characterize the Word, for it may be that the life was human life, in which case the Word was Creator or instrument in creating human life that shines amid darkness. What is it in the human race that "shines in the darkness" so strongly that "the darkness has not overcome it"? The light might be humanity's spiritual dimension. It might be the rational dimension. Of course, the life that was the light of the human race may refer to the life of some other entity—that is, the Word—that shines for humanity and protects it from the darkness. The Word could then be both divine and human. Metaphoric language, in brief, is not always reducible to one meaning or one layer of meanings.

When we read John 1:14, some of the questions above may be resolved: "the Word became flesh." Flesh renders what was with and what was God as human, "dwelling among us," and clearly evidencing "the glory as of the Father's only Son / Full of grace and truth." The Word seemingly was with God from the beginning, shares in God's divinity, and also seems like the Son of God. As the Son and as God, the Word shared in creating life and was a means of renewing life—human life that shone amid darkness—by being a beacon of divine light and truth.

Having said all of this, we still have not addressed the central question: Why is the Son of God called God's "Word"? This may be the way divinity accommodates truth to human beings. It may be that God speaks to humans only through chosen ones such as the Son; the Son's words and actions may allow God to speak to the human race. The Son's words and actions may be the means by which God makes humans—otherwise blind amid the darkness—aware of divine truth or light.

We might suggest much more about these opening lines—indeed, I have not presumed to analyze them as sacred text embodying divine truth, as a theologian might. I have not considered allusions to the Old Testament or even the contextual connotations of other words that comprise the verse and modify the central tenor and vehicles already mentioned. For instance, darkness—in the context of God's Word taking on flesh to bring light to humans—might very well refer to the darkness of sin, of nonrational life, of rational life blind to divinity, and so on. Poetry and metaphor, in short, generate multiple levels of meaning.

For centuries, readers of sacred and profane poetry alike accepted such rich depth and complexity of meaning as the nature of metaphoric, connotative, contextually shaped language. This very depth and complexity drew readers back to the same works repeatedly. Each visit rewarded them with new insights into the authors' visions. To be sure, some "insights" proved to be incorrect or improbable. Interpretations of particular poems and novels sometimes did not stand the tests to which other literary critics put them.

Thus, an interpretation that took literally the irony and satire in Swift's *Modest Proposal* was incorrect. An interpretation of Wordsworth's *Intimations Ode* that found wanton sexuality in "the Children [who] sport upon the shore" (l. 166) was judged at the least improbable. And very few academics or students would have quibbled with these assessments. Multiple levels of complex meaning did not provide a rationale for relativism among interpretations. Interpreters did not resort to power to dislodge other interpretations; very often they saw themselves as highlighting complementary views that incrementally were progressing toward a fuller appreciation of a work's meaning.

All this has changed as a significant number of modern intellectuals have denied that human reason can shed light on the meaning of words and texts. Not only do they deny that reason can comprehend the truth or meaning of metaphoric, connotative texts, but they have extended their claims to expository prose as well. Literary historians refer to these intellectuals as *postmodernists* and to the movement characterized by their views of knowledge and of the meaning of words as *postmodernism* (Barton and Hudson 147–49).

Postmodernists specifically deny to authors, on the one hand, any ability to fix or control the meaning of their texts; they also deny to readers, on the other hand, any ability to comprehend the truth or meaning of texts. In this intellectual context at the millennium, Catholicism must take and hold on to a countercultural stance that insists on reason's ability to know the essences of real things that exist separately from the mind, especially the meaning of words, for without such a stance, there can be no truth in the Word of God. To establish this point, I first review current notions of epistemology and their implications for comprehending words and for Catholicism; then, I suggest what the countercultural stance entails and why it is reasonable.

POSTMODERNISTS AND THE MEANING OF TEXTS

In *Fides et Ratio*, Pope John Paul II acknowledges the challenges that postmodern claims pose for Catholicism and any text-based religions. He is upset that "some scholars . . . [in the fields of hermeneutics and the analysis of language] tend to stop short at the question of how reality is understood and expressed, without going further to see whether reason can discover its essence," for "in such a frame of mind [we 'can discover'] the confirmation of our present crisis of confidence in the powers of reason" (84). The upshot of this modern crisis is that the Word of God cannot shed any light on human darkness. Rather, "the word of God . . . would not be capable of saying anything about God. The interpretation of the word cannot merely keep referring us to one interpretation after another, without ever leading us to a statement which is simply true; otherwise, there would be no Revelation of God, but only the expression of human notions about God and what God presumably thinks of us" (84). Though the pope may believe that interpretations of texts "cannot merely keep referring us to one interpretation after another, without ever leading us to a statement which is simply true," postmodernists believe that this is precisely the situation in which we find ourselves.

According to historian Gertrude Himmelfarb, "The mainspring of postmodernism is a radical—an absolute, one might say—relativism, skepticism, and subjectivism that rejects . . . the very idea of truth. For the postmodernist, there is no truth, no knowledge, no objectivity, no reason, and, ultimately, no reality" ("Revolution" 201). Skepticism so permeates contemporary discussion of the nature of human knowledge that "no philosophical account of knowledge can be accepted as true," thus breeding "a certain cynicism and even nihilism about the quest for objective knowledge" (Sweetman, "Introduction," 2). As a result, postmodernists call into question all particular beings, including all written documents—historical, literary, legal, theological, scientific, and even business. Relying heavily on the work of deconstructionists such as Derrida, postmodernists deny that particular beings or identities exist independently; rather, "identities are simply constructs of the mind, and essentially of language." The identity or meaning of a text is thus dependent on the reader and social context (Sweetman, "Deconstruction," 236). In other words, textual meaning is relative, and different readers' constructions of textual meaning are individual and subjective. By extension, mental constructions of any phenomenon are relative and subjective.

Stanley Fish asserts these postmodernist notions about textual meaning in his appropriately titled book *Is There a Text in This Class?*

> Indeed, the text as an entity independent of interpretation and (ideally) responsible for its career drops out and is replaced by the texts that emerge as the consequence of our interpretive activities. There are still formal patterns, but they do not lie innocently in the world; rather, they are themselves constituted by an interpretive act. The facts one points to are still there *(in a sense that would not be consoling to an objectivist)* but only as a consequence of the interpretive (man-made) model that has called them into being. The relationship between interpretation and text is thus reversed: interpretive strategies are not put into execution after reading; they are the shape of reading, and because they are the shape of reading, they give texts their shape, making them rather than, as is usually assumed, arising from them. (13, my italics)

Fish asserts that readers create the texts that they read and bases this assertion on his assumption that readers and writers are members of "interpretive communities . . . made up of those who share interpretive strategies not for reading, but for writing texts, for constituting their properties. In other words, these strategies exist prior to the act of reading and therefore determine the shape of what is read rather than, as is usually assumed, the other way round" (14). An individual is literally determined by one or another interpretive community in what he or she can think, "as much a product of that community (acting as an extension of it) as the meanings it enables him [or her] to produce" (14).

As a result, interpretations of metaphoric texts can no longer move "toward a more accurate account of a fixed and stable entity," nor can we judge interpretations based on "facts that are independently specified" (365–66). Rather, interpretation is a matter of persuasion and power: "to establish by political and persuasive means (they are the same thing) the set of interpretive assumptions from the vantage of which the evidence (and the facts and the intentions and everything else) will hereafter be specifiable" (15–16). Indeed, one interpretation can replace another only by power—not by rational discourse: "change occurs when one perspective dislodges another" (356).

In essence, Fish and his postmodern followers leave writers and readers in Hobbes's state of nature, where competition among representatives of different interpretive communities really is a state of war "of every [hu]man against every [hu]man" (185), each endeavoring "to destroy or subdue [or dislodge] one an other [sic]" (184). Reason cannot escape from what determines it, for either Hobbes or the postmodernists. Reason cannot examine critically and objectively the nature of an interpretive community or the appetites, nor can it then infer that what the interpretive community imposes by power or what the appetites desire as pleasureful are incorrect or immoral. As both Fish and Hobbes indicate, in nature and in interpretive communities, "The notions of Right and Wrong, Justice and Injustice have there no place" (Hobbes 188). Only the power of persuasion or physical force obtains.

Extending this line of thinking, Lyotard insists that texts are the means by which power structures maintain power: "in the discourse of today's financial backers of research, the only credible goal is power. Scientists, technicians, and instruments are purchased not to find truth, but to augment power" (46). In fact, "knowledge and power are simply two sides of the same question" (8–9). Knowledge for such skeptics is really nothing more than discourse, "a construction of language as the instrument of culture. The consequence of this is that, since each culture evolves and authorizes its own language games, our knowledge is, in the last analysis, culturally bound . . . in such a way that we are effectively shut off from real things" (Hancock, "Critique," 246).

In brief, postmodernists lock us into prisons of subjective perception that prevent us from knowing reality as it is. Attempts at conveying our subjective perceptions of reality in language are mere discourse or game. One person's perceptions and language games are equal to any other person's in the resulting relativism—unless by power individuals can impose their will on others. One "reading has no more legitimacy than any other reading if any reading is permissible; it cannot be morally better, or textually more appropriate, or philosophically more acceptable than the other alternatives" (Sweetman, "Postmodernism," 15). If one reading of a text or one perception of reality is judged superior to another, postmodernists would be acknowledging that there are objective truths and that we can know them. Of course, the irony of postmodernism is that its proponents do just this. They claim to know as true that people cannot know reality and that there is no objective truth.

At one extreme, reading theory about how the memory stores knowledge and processes texts lends itself to the postmodernist view of indeterminate texts and subjective construction of textual meaning. Because, according to the predominant reading theory, readers employ schemata—frameworks of prior knowledge stored hierarchically in long-term memory—in processing texts, "meaning is not in the message." "While the idea of autonomous text has considerable social utility, it would appear to be wrong or, at least, to have maladaptive side effects. Text is gobbledygook unless the reader possesses an interpretive framework to breathe meaning into it" (Anderson, "The Notion of Schemata," 422–23). Anderson at least acknowledges that "mine is explicitly a relativistic view of language and language comprehension." To his credit, he admits of "a danger in relativism and subjectivism." The dangers he feared in 1977 are all quite real today: "There could be serious consequences if well-meaning technocrats caused a generation of American school teachers and children to believe that any sincere interpretation of a message were as good as another" (428). Actually, the danger is worse, because teachers and humanists themselves have supplanted the technocrats.

In this context, it should not be surprising that historians even ridicule concern for facts as a fetish, as if facts are much less important—if one accepts facts as real—than one's perceptions and one's feelings about them (Himmelfarb, *Abyss*, 141–42). For instance, a controversial study on pedophilia concluded that the label *child sexual abuse* ought not to be applied indiscriminately to all adult-child sexual encounters. "The indiscriminate use of this term and related terms such as *victim* and *perpetrator* has been criticized because of concerns about scientific validity" (Rind, Tromovitch, and Bauserman 22), as if individuals cannot know objectively the nature of such sexual acts and the fitting words for them. Rather, we should "focus on the young person's perception of his or her willingness to participate and his or her reactions to the experience" (46). Postmodernism has indeed altered the landscape of knowledge and truth.

Despite the mountains of data, including eyewitness accounts, that tell us that six million Jews were murdered in the Holocaust, postmodernism provides the bases for denying it occurred (Himmelfarb, *Abyss*, 143–46). In the face of incontrovertible, objectively known factual data, postmodernists have even attempted to explain away, to deconstruct, the "indeterminate" texts that express the anti-Semitic filth of the late Paul de Man, a postmodern guru in this country (Lehman 212–19).

Postmodernists deny the possibility of objective knowledge, fixed or stable textual meaning, rational discourse and reflection, and traditional morality. Postmodernists deny all that Catholicism professes, especially the truth of its sacred texts and the texts of those who interpret sacred texts. In this intellectual context, Catholicism must adopt and proclaim widely the opposition view Pope John Paul II set out in *Fides et Ratio* and that a number of other modern thinkers profess. Catholicism must proclaim its conviction that reason can know objects that exist independently of the mind, including the meaning of texts.

TRUTH, REASON, AND CATHOLICISM

To begin, Catholicism must commit itself to "the idea of knowledge that guided the universities for almost a millennium" (Willard 6). This idea, according to Dallas Willard, "is one according to which to know is to be able to think of things as they are, as distinct from how they only seem or are taken to be, and to be able to do so on an appropriate basis of experience or thought" (6). To arrive at this commitment, people must, like Willard, choose classical realism—a "critical and rational . . . conviction that the knower is immediately aware of the external world" (Hancock, "Epilogue," 259). Simply put, the classical realist begins with the conviction that the external world of objects exists independently of the mind and that the mind can know them.

Objectivism or realism rejects perception or "what seems to be" as an inadequate replacement for knowledge—for example, knowledge of a sexual act. Objectivists would especially find a child's perception less than adequate. They would, by contrast, strive to know the particulars or the nature of the act in and of itself. They would come to know objectively that children—perception aside—cannot willingly participate in sexual relationships with adults. Objectivists would know that *child sexual abuse* denotes particulars—that is, the nature of the act or the acts. In this case, the fact that an adult had sexual relations with a child—or even "a mature 15-year old" (Rind, Tromovitch, and Bauserman 23)—constitutes the very act(s) to which the term *child sexual abuse* fittingly applies. Objectivists believe that humans can know what constitutes rape, sodomy, sexual harassment, spousal abuse, racial discrimination, and so on. From this perspective, objectivists would know—regardless of the child's reactions to the experience—that society's reaction ought to be moral revulsion and outrage.

As David Lehman concludes his indictment of De Man and postmodern thought, he emphasizes how vital it is "to remind oneself of the dangers that ensue when metaphors substitute for facts, when words lose their meaning, and when signifiers and signifieds part company" (243)—for example, when the terms *pedophilia* and *child sexual abuse* part company with child-adult sexual relations.

Human capacities of thought or reason can also go beyond empirical knowledge of the external world. Indeed, "Knowledge itself, and most of the things worth knowing, are not sense-perceptible" (Willard 11). As Pope John Paul II puts it in *Fides et Ratio*, "It is the nature of the human being to seek the truth. This search looks not only to the attainment of truths which are partial, empirical or scientific. . . . [The people's] search looks towards an ulterior truth which would explain the meaning of life. . . . Thanks to the inherent capacities of thought, man is able to encounter and recognize a truth of this kind" (33).

To a greater or lesser extent, in pursuit of truth, humans find themselves trusting to what others have to say about truth—theologians, for example. Human reason, from a Christian view, is fallen "wounded and weakened by sin" (John Paul II 51). Consequently, no individual can hope to arrive at absolute truth—divine truth—on his or her own. "This is why no historical form of philosophy can legitimately claim to embrace the totality of truth" (John Paul II 51). And this is why the pope advises theologians of the dangers "inherent in seeking to derive the truth of Sacred Scripture from the use of one method alone, ignoring the need for a more comprehensive exegesis which enables the exegete, together with the whole Church, to arrive at the full sense of the texts" (55). Catholicism, then, looks for a good deal of the truth in its sacred texts and in the commentaries on these texts—within the constraints of Sacred Tradition and the teaching authority of the Magisterium. In both Scripture and commentary, Catholicism looks for truth in words: it looks for the truth of God's Word in human words.

Words stand as a prima facie case that important knowledge is not sense perceptible. Were this not the case, as Willard notes, all that books and literature present us would be reduced to "the physics of pages" (11). The body of knowledge that has grown up around the reading process, moreover, provides more than ample evidence (1) that the words on a page and the mental representations of the meaning of words differ and (2) that the mental process of comprehending the meanings of words on a page escapes empirical observation. And these comments are as true for metaphoric language as they are for denotative language.

Fish and other postmodernists (from Derrida and De Man to Lyotard and Anderson) variously deny words any stable meaning outside of interpretive communities, insisting "that as each reader reads a text differently, somehow the text itself is different for each reader" (Dasenbrock 7). In this way, postmodernists deny readers the ability to comprehend texts objectively and, thus, to learn from them. Postmodernists trap readers in a conversation with themselves, unable to share others' thoughts in print (Dasenbrock 16–17).

Catholicism must challenge this postmodernist position on words on the same grounds as it challenges postmodern skepticism. As the Roman Catholic Church must counter the determinism of interpretive communities by committing itself to a realism that frees reason to know extramental objects, so it must counter narcissistic and solipsistic notions of how individuals create texts in a dialogue with themselves.

Reed Dasenbrock takes on Fish and the others directly by examining the experience of reading literary texts:

> as we actually interpret, we encounter anomalies, sentences that don't seem to agree with what we hold true. Our immediate reaction when we encounter difference is to refuse that difference. . . . But the interesting moments are when this doesn't work so well, when we realize that what we are interpreting does express beliefs different from our own. This for me is the most important reason to read and to study literature, to break out of our own circle of beliefs and assumptions and to encounter another point of view. The key issue on which Fish and I disagree is whether this is possible or not. (16)

For Dasenbrock (as for Willard and realists generally), readers can see texts as different from them, as objects independent of their reasons, and they can comprehend these objects when they contain propositions radically different from their own. Readers can acknowledge the truth or falsity of these propositions when warranted, even when they come from different cultures (17). As the pope insists, "it is possible to move from the historical and contingent circumstances in which texts developed to the truth which they express, a truth transcending those circumstances"; "Truth can never be confined to time and culture" (*Fides et Ratio* 95). These claims are demonstrated every time someone reads a literary work such as John Dryden's "Absalom and Achitophel," knowing the biblical and Miltonic parallels to the contingent circumstances of the Exclusion Crisis in England: factions, led by Shaftesbury, tried to exclude the Catholic James from succeeding his brother King Charles II; these factions incited the Duke of Monmouth, illegitimate son of Charles, to lead a rebellion. Despite these circumstances, one can still get at time-less truths about political machinations, virtue, self-interest, the public good, politically devious rhetoric; and one can still be caught up short by Dryden's antidemocratic thoughts.

If we turn to reader theory, we find very much what Dasen-brock has argued, including data that suggest just how exposi-tory texts can enhancé reader comprehension. We shall discover that readers can bring personal frameworks of prior knowledge to written documents—frameworks that influence their compre-hension—and still comprehend the meanings intended by writ-ers; that readers do come to know the truth or meaning embodied in the words on a page. We shall also find out that writers can—with hard work—provide helpful cues and con-straining contexts to make it easier for readers to comprehend texts. We shall, in fact, find that reading theory often stands di-rectly within the long tradition of philosophical realism in claim-ing truth, knowledge, and objectivity for its propositions.

Reading theory has arisen to explain decades of data gathered in experimental observations of the reading process. Although no researcher can observe what goes on inside of the reader's mind during text processing, the results of experiments have al-lowed various explanations to emerge. The explanations center on the way long-term memory and short-term memory function in reading. For our purposes, we shall focus on long-term mem-ory, which, according to the predominant theory of the past sev-eral decades, seemingly stores information gleaned from texts in hierarchical frameworks or schemata. When readers encounter information in texts, especially new or unfamiliar information, they actively integrate the unfamiliar into the previously known. Sometimes the new information may be so utterly unfamiliar that it forces the reader to restructure or fashion new schemata (see Schallert, "The Significance of Knowledge: Synthesis of Re-search Related to Schema Theory").

Bransford insists that "Since a major goal of education is to help students develop new skills and knowledge—to help them become able to understand things that they could not under-stand previously—the issue of schema construction or schema acquisition is extremely important" (263). However, according to Bransford, some schema theorists such as Anderson, cited earlier, stop short of discussing schema acquisition. Anderson discusses instead schema activation, leaving readers trapped inside of their own prior knowledge much as Fish did: "The schema that will be brought to bear on a text depends upon the reader's age, sex, race, religion, nationality, occupation—in short, it depends upon the reader's culture" ("Role of the Reader's Schema" 245).

Despite Anderson's consistent postmodernism, a good number of schema theorists exhibit classical realism at the heart of their experiments. In contrast to novices, experts in given fields come prepared "with rich sets of pattern-indexed schemata that guides [sic] problem interpretation and solution" (Jonassen, Beissner, and Yacci 10). Nonetheless, because "learning consists of building new knowledge structures by constructing new nodes and interrelating them with existing nodes and with each other" (9), novices can comprehend new data—albeit with more difficulty than the expert.

Schallert qualifies extreme implications of schema theory that might suggest that meaning resides in the reader only: "Meaning is formed as a result of the dynamic interaction between existing abstract knowledge structures and the clues available from the message. The result of this interaction is a particularized, concretized representation" (27). That is, readers construct both a mental representation of the textbase that "reflects the coherence relations among the propositions in a text and their organization" and a mental representation of the situation described in the text. Integration of the mental representation of the situation into existing schemata may entail "either the updating of an existing situation model [that is, schema] or the construction of a new one on the basis of the information obtained from the text" (Kintsch 88–89).

But the fact that readers' schemata interact with textual cues and perhaps at times miss or distort the cues does not deny that the cues are there or can be known. As Haviland and Clark emphasize, well-crafted linguistic information or cues come in contexts, not in ambiguous isolation. And "In paragraphs, such context effects have a tendency to snowball" (512), constraining readers' schemata from rambling too far from a text's meaning. Should readers wander too far because of the limits of their schemata, then we can say that they have not really gotten at the meaning of a text; we don't merely conclude that readers create their own meanings. Should readers and decision makers, for instance, misread a business report, stakeholders will gladly set them right. To the point of this chapter, if theologians stray in reading John's Gospel, the Magisterium of the Church as well as other theologians will set them right (John Paul II 50).

Schema research actually presumes that readers can comprehend the meaning of words in a text objectively, can construct accurate representation of the textbase and of the situation in the text. Researchers repeatedly set out to measure statistically the ease of comprehending specific texts. In nearly every case, researchers presume that the research subjects can understand the meaning of the words objectively and that the researchers can as well. For example, Lipson's measures of comprehension note that "each passage had associated with it six recognition items, one for each category [four categories of inference and two categories of recognition items]. This resulted in eight exemplars of each recognition type, one for each of the eight passages. *These 48 recognition items were then paired to a comparable, but incorrect, statement and constituted the 48 recognition pairs used to assess both prior knowledge and post-reading comprehension*" (247, my italics). Readers are not trapped within their own subjective schemata as Anderson comes very close to claiming, for they can recognize textual cues about meaning within constraining contexts.

Novices in wine tasting, moreover, may not be as adept as an expert at comprehending text content about taste or bouquet, but they may be superior to professional tasters in processing or recognizing knowledge structures in texts. That is, *expert* and *novice* may denote reader differences independent of content knowledge. Expert readers have far richer sets of schemata for "author biases, intentions, and goals" as well as for "text structure," helping them to determine textual importance more readily and to "identify and organize information" more readily. Expert readers are also more adept at using prior content knowledge to get at present textual content (Dole et al. 243).

Comprehension of texts will vary, in part, according to differences among readers. But independently of reader expertise in text content or text structure, some texts can make processing

easier—especially for the novice—by making knowledge structures more evident. And first among helpful knowledge structures are categories of data. Research demonstrates a category
effect in various cognitive activities whereby people process
data more efficiently when they know certain items do or do not
belong to specific categories (Dixon 286–87). For example, when
a person is told (orally or in writing) that the only important
data belong to the category of mammals, then that person more
readily passes over irrelevant data on reptiles or insects while
more easily detecting and retaining data on humans, cows,
whales, etc.

These structures or categories very much parallel the schemata of long-term memory: "structural knowledge, like schemata, is a useful construct or metaphor for describing the ways
that humans construct and store knowledge." In short, "If structural knowledge is integral to learning and performing higher
order mental operations like problem solving, then performance
should be improved by conveying the structure of information"
(Jonassen, Beissner, and Yacci 12). Thus, in preparing texts, writers ought to be organizing data into categories to address reader
needs in the comprehension process. Within categories, furthermore, we know that writers can enhance learning from texts by
beginning with an initial paragraph that previews the main
points of the category, closing with a summary and conclusion
paragraph, employing headings before each main point, and
using transitional paragraphs (Lee 138–39, 141–44). Researchers
have also pointed out other textual cues that help readers: advance organizers (Mayer 376–82), topic sentences (Selzer 81–82),
antecedent references in successive sentences in a paragraph
(Haviland and Clark 514–20). Again, in these experiments, the
researchers assume that they can know the meaning of the various texts they present to students, and they conclude—based on
measurable data—that the students variously comprehended
the meaning of texts and that some texts are easier to comprehend than others.

Closing Thoughts

I have emphasized that reason can know the external world and
especially the world of texts. With the pope and other thinkers,

I view postmodernism as a pernicious force, opposed to what Roman Catholicism professes regarding the meaning of its sacred texts and interpretations of these texts. But reason alone cannot rise to the divine truth of Scripture: "The results of reasoning may in fact be true, but these results acquire their true meaning only if they are set within the larger horizon of faith. . . . [H]uman beings attain truth by way of reason because, enlightened by faith, they discover the deeper meaning of all things and most especially of their own existence" (John Paul II 20).

I have focused primarily on text comprehension because that is my area of expertise and because, in today's intellectual climate, it must take primacy. That is, Catholicism rests upon "the word of God which she has received in faith" (John Paul II 7), but words have been attacked as unstable, leaving individual readers and interpretive communities to displace authoritative interpretations by power and persuasion. It is urgent for us to see that "Faith clearly presupposes that human language is capable of expressing divine and transcendent reality" (John Paul II 84). It is equally urgent that human language be able to express truthful interpretations of sacred scripture. I have suggested that realism is the bedrock view of the world that redeems "the wisdom of words" from indeterminacy. And although it is "the Word of Wisdom"—John's Word become flesh—"which Saint Paul offers as the criterion of both truth and salvation," the Word cannot shed light on human darkness without "the wisdom of words" (John Paul II 23).

WORKS CITED

Anderson, Richard C. "The Notion of Schemata and the Educational Enterprise: General Discussion of the Conference." In *Schooling and the Acquisition of Knowledge*, edited by R. C. Anderson and R. J. Spiro, 415–31. Hillsdale, N.J.: Lawrence Erlbaum, 1977.

———. "Role of the Reader's Schema in Comprehension, Learning, and Memory." In *Learning to Read in American Schools: Basal Readers and Content Texts*, edited by R. C. Anderson, J.

Osborn, and R. J. Tierney, 243–57. Hillsdale, N.J.: Lawrence Erlbaum, 1984.

Barton, Edwin J., and Glenda A. Hudson. *A Contemporary Guide to Literary Terms, with Strategies for Writing Essays about Literature*. Boston: Houghton Mifflin, 1997.

Bransford, John D. "Schema Activation and Schema Acquisition: Comments on Richard C. Anderson's Remarks." In *Learning to Read in American Schools: Basal Readers and Content Texts*, edited by R. C. Anderson, J. Osborn, and R. J. Tierney, 259–82. Hillsdale, N.J.: Lawrence Erlbaum, 1984.

Dasenbrock, Reed W. "Do We Write the Text We Read?" *College English* 53, no. 1 (1991): 7–18.

Dixon, Peter. "The Category Effect in Visual Detection and Partial Report." *Perception and Psychophysics* 38, no. 3 (1985): 286–95.

Dole, Janice A., Gerald G. Duffy, Laura R. Roehler, and P. David Pearson. "Moving from the Old to the New: Research on Reading Comprehension Instruction." *Review of Educational Research* 61, no. 2 (1991): 239–64.

Fish, Stanley. *Is There a Text in This Class? The Authority of Interpretive Communities*. Cambridge, Mass.: Harvard University Press, 1980.

Hancock, Curtis L. "A Critique of Social Construct Theory: Relativism's Latest Fashion." In *The Failure of Modernism: The Cartesian Legacy and Contemporary Pluralism*, edited by Brendan Sweetman, 241–58. Washington, D.C.: Catholic University Press, 1999.

———. "Epilogue: A Counterfeit Choice." In *The Failure of Modernism*, edited by Brendan Sweetman, 259–62. Washington, D.C.: Catholic University Press, 1999.

Haviland, Susan E., and Herbert H. Clark. "What's New? Acquiring New Information as a Process in Comprehension." *Journal of Verbal Learning and Verbal Behavior* 13 (1974): 512–21.

Himmelfarb, Gertrude. *On Looking into the Abyss: Untimely Thoughts on Culture and Society*. New York: Vantage, 1995.

———. "Revolution in the Library." *The American Scholar* (spring 1997): 197–204.

Hobbes, Thomas. *Leviathan*. 1651. Edited by C. B. Macpherson. Middlesex, England: Pelican Classics, 1974.

John Paul II. *Fides et Ratio.* September 14, 1998.

Jonassen, David H., Katherine Beissner, and Michael Yacci. *Structural Knowledge: Techniques for Representing, Conveying, and Acquiring Structural Knowledge.* Hillsdale, N.J.: Lawrence Erlbaum, 1993.

Kintsch, Walter. "Learning from Text." *Cognition and Instruction* 3, no. 2 (1986): 87–108.

Lee, Wayne. "Supra-Paragraph Prose Structure: Its Specification, Perception, and Effects on Learning." *Psychological Reports* 17 (1965): 135–44.

Lehman, David. *Signs of the Times, Deconstruction, and the Fall of Paul De Man.* New York: Poseidon, 1991.

Lipson, Marjorie Youmans. "Learning New Information from Text: The Role of Prior Knowledge and Reading Ability." *Journal of Reading Behavior* 14, no. 3 (1982): 243–61.

Lyotard, Jean-François. *The Postmodern Condition: A Report on Knowledge.* 1979. Translated by Geoff Bennington and Brian Massumi. Theory and History of Literature, vol. 10. Minneapolis: University of Minnesota Press, 1997.

Mayer, Richard E. "Can Advance Organizers Influence Meaningful Learning?" *Review of Educational Research* 49 (1979): 371–83.

Rind, Bruce, Philip Tromovitch, and Robert Bauserman. "A Meta-Analytic Examination of Assumed Properties of Child Sexual Abuse Using College Samples." *Psychological Bulletin* 124, no. 1 (1998): 22–53.

Schallert, Diane Lemonnier. "The Significance of Knowledge: A Synthesis of Research Related to Schema Theory." In *Reading Expository Material,* edited by W. Otto and S. White, 13–48. New York: Academic, 1982.

Selzer, Jack. "What Constitutes a 'Readable' Technical Style?" In *New Essays in Technical and Scientific Communication: Research, Theory, and Practice,* edited by P. V. Anderson, R. J. Bruckmann, and C. R. Miller, 71–89. Farmingdale, N.Y.: Baywood, 1983.

Sweetman, Brendan. "The Deconstruction of Western Metaphysics: Derrida and Maritain on Identity." In *Postmodernism and Christian Philosophy,* edited by R. T. Ciapalo, 230–47. Washington, D.C.: Catholic University Press, 1997.

———. "Introduction." In *The Failure of Modernism,* edited by B.

Sweetman, 1–9. Washington, D.C.: Catholic University Press, 1999.

———. "Postmodernism, Derrida, and *Differánce:* A Critique." *International Philosophical Quarterly* 39, no. 1 (1999): 5–18.

Willard, Dallas. "The Unhinging of the American Mind: Derrida as Pretext." In *European Philosophy and the American Academy,* edited by B. Smith, 3–20. LaSalle, Ill.: Monist Library of Philosophy, 1994.

THREE
Church and Culture

5

Inculturation, Signs of the Times, and the Rapidly Changing Culture

Wilfred LaCroix, S.J.

POPE PAUL VI wrote that "the split between the Gospel and culture is without a doubt the tragedy of our time" (20). We might begin here wondering, "Why is this split such a bad thing?" (There were, of course, historical causes for this split, especially in the eighteenth and nineteenth centuries.)

We must add that the pope was referring only to the split between the Western European culture and the Gospel. There has been as yet no real unity in the relation of the Gospel and Asian or African cultures that could have a subsequent split.

In Africa, there is a desire to free the Gospel from a colonial legacy, which undervalued the quality of indigenous African cultural values, and to bring it into a more profound contact with African life. The Vatican's Pontifical Council for Culture has just recently acknowledged the positive values in the various African cultures, values such as "a sense of family, love and respect for life, veneration of ancestors, a sense of solidarity and community, and respect for the chief and elders" (Pontifical Council for Culture 19).

Asia, the Pontifical Council acknowledges, is a different matter. "Asia as a whole may well still appear unaffected by the message of Christ, but is that not chiefly because Christianity is still perceived there as a foreign religion introduced by Westerners, which has not been sufficiently adapted, thought through and lived in the cultures of Asia?" (20). Aloysius Pieris, a Sri Lankan Jesuit, offers the analogy of a tree planted in a pot filled with European earth, not with native Asian soil. He calls it a "stunted bonsai" (Pieris 53).

Pope John Paul II has recently written of Asia's many expressions of spirituality and mysticism with emphasis on holiness, self-denial, chastity, universal love, a love for peace, prayer and contemplation, bliss in God, and compassion. He sees these expressions as very much alive in Asian cultures, perhaps especially in India (*Fides et Ratio* 72). Of late, the pope has maintained a general insistence that the Gospel message must be open to all cultures and made accessible to every human person through a process of *inculturation.*

The New Use of the Term *Inculturation*

Let us start with *culture.* Its literal meaning indicates preparing ground for growth. The analogous use is that which prepares people to interpret and organize their experience. The Greeks called it *paideia,* the Romans *humanitas.* Culture is the human air we breathe, the human ground we tread and build on, the images we use to express ourselves and to relate to others and to our world.

So what is *inculturation* of the Gospel? Think of Pieris's image of a tree planted in a pot filled with European soil and a tree planted in native Asian soil. Or think of an image that Carlos Valles, a Jesuit in India, related of the Gospel as a branch grafted onto a southern European tree or as the same branch grafted onto a southern Asian tree (Valles 59–60). As the tree or the branch later grows, it takes on good elements of its host soil or its host tree, while simultaneously enriching the soil or the tree with its special characteristics.

Analogously, then, the Gospel, in the dynamic of inculturation, introduces something new into the culture, and in the same union the culture brings something new to the richness of the Gospel.

The force of the analogy is that the Gospel must grow in a culture in order to be able to interpret and organize the everyday experience of those in that culture. John Paul II says this explicitly: "Through inculturation the Church makes the Gospel incarnate in different cultures and at the same time introduces people, together with their cultures, into her own community. She transmits to them her own values, at the same time taking the good elements that already exist in them and renewing them from within" (*Redemptoris Missio* 52). Inculturation must take place on a two-way street.

THE SPIRIT AND INCULTURATION

The assumption behind inculturation is not that astonishing, but it has proven elusive. It is simply that God is always active in the world and God's work is bound to no single culture. In his encyclical *Redemptoris Missio* (The Mission of the Redeemer), John Paul II says: "[The Spirit's] presence and activity are universal, limited neither by space nor time." He reinforces this claim with three quotes from Vatican II (see *Redemptoris Missio* 28): (1) "it is the Spirit who sows the 'seeds of the word' present in various customs and cultures" (*Lumen Gentium* 17); (2) "the Spirit of God, with marvelous foresight, directs the course of the ages and renews the face of the earth" (*Gaudium et Spes* 26); and (3) the risen Christ "is now at work in human hearts through the strength of his Spirit" (*Gaudium et Spes* 38).

These quotations indicate that the presence and activity of the Spirit of Christ are unlimited. *Yet, the official expression of the Gospel has been bound to central-southern European culture since the start of the modern period.*

So what could make us think in today's rapidly changing global culture that there is an opening for a new and successful inculturation? I suggest it is precisely now that we can appreciate as never before the need and the possibility for such inculturation. In his talk opening Vatican Council II, Pope John XXIII expressed the principle for such a suggestion:

> In the daily exercise of our pastoral office, we sometimes have to listen, much to our regret, to voices of persons who, though burning with zeal, are not endowed with too much sense of discretion or measure. In these modern times they can see nothing but prevarication and ruin. They say our era, in comparison with past eras, is getting worse and they behave as though they had learned

nothing from history, which is, none the less, the teacher of life. They behave as though at the time of former Councils everything was a full triumph for the Christian idea and life and for proper religious liberty. We feel we must disagree with these prophets of doom who are always forecasting disaster, as though the end of the world were at hand. In the present order of things, Divine Providence is leading us to a new order of human relations which, by people's own efforts and even beyond their very expectations, are directed toward the fulfillment of God's superior and inscrutable designs. And everything, even human differences, leads to the greater good of the Church. (426–27)

Accepting the pope's confidence that God is leading us in ways beyond our expectations toward fulfilling God's inscrutable designs, the council's members reemphasized the *duty of recognizing the signs of the times* for what they are: "To carry out such a task, the Church has always had the duty of scrutinizing the *signs of the times* and of interpreting them in the light of the gospel. Thus, *in language intelligible to each generation,* she can respond to the perennial questions which people ask about this present life and the life to come, and about the relationship of the one to the other" (*Gaudium et Spes* 4: 201–2, italics mine). Note here the order: first, recognize and scrutinize the signs of the times, then interpret them in light of the Gospel; second, speak to people "in language intelligible to each generation," which has to include using references and images appropriate to each culture at each place and time. The council also said:

Today, *the human race is passing through a new stage of its history.* Profound and rapid changes are spreading by degrees around the whole world. Triggered by the intelligence and creative energies of humans, these changes recoil upon them, upon their decisions and desires, both individual and collective, and upon their manner of thinking and acting with respect to things and to people. Hence we can already speak of a *true social and cultural transformation,* one which has repercussions on their religious life as well (*Gaudium et Spes* 4: 202, italics mine).

What then might be the main features of this social and cultural transformation?

The council suggests that one sign of transformation is that "the human race has passed from a rather static concept of reality to a more dynamic, evolutionary one" (*Gaudium et Spes* 5). (Teilhard de Chardin once commented that with humans on the scene, for the first time evolution involves choice!) By their efforts, "they are unfolding the Creator's work, . . . to the realization in history of the divine plan" (*Gaudium et Spes* 5). Consequently, "it is an error for people to see the works produced by their own talent and energy to be in opposition to God's power, or that we stand as a kind of rival to the Creator" (*Gaudium et Spes* 34).

A second sign of social and cultural transformation is the compressing of most of us together in our work, in our sense of time and space, and in our living.

In our work, the world capitalist economy involves both global interdependence in the division of labor and the worldwide diffusion of machine technologies. This combination has forced us all to confront how we live our lives in connection with the lives of others in very distant parts of the world (*Gaudium et Spes* 23). In our sense of time and space, the compressing comes mainly by the technologies of communication. In our living, the compressing comes with the rapidly increasing urbanization. In 1900, roughly 5 percent of the world lived in cities (with a population greater than 100,000). Between 1950 and 1995, the number of cities in the industrially developed core countries with population greater than one million went from 49 to 112. During the same forty-five years, the number of cities in the periphery went from 34 to 213 (Linden 53).

A third sign of transformation might be the changing makeup of the Roman Catholic Church itself. Its numbers are coming to be mostly in peripheral countries, mostly among the poor and mostly young. And these young have a growing sense of dignity and freedom (*Dignitatis Humanae* 1).

A fourth sign of transformation might be the growing sense of a Church as truly Catholic, as truly a World Church. Karl Rahner suggests that this is a deep message coming from Vatican II. Some of us see the incredible travel work of John Paul II as *physically symbolizing* this world unity and as a complement to his encyclicals *Redemptoris Missio* and *Fides et Ratio*.

Now we might explore what guides we might have for inculturation.

Have the Followers of Jesus Done This Before?

It would seem wise if, before getting to inculturation today, we looked briefly on efforts to inculturate the Gospel by earlier followers of Jesus. But even prior to this look, there is a more primordial question whose answer must guide our understanding of inculturation of the Gospel: Did Jesus himself, who insisted that he was sent to the people of Israel, inculturate his message as he came to them?

The answer: he had to. That is the only way humans can grasp the significance of the message in their lives. First of all, he became incarnate as a male Jew to the Jews, who would not have given ear to a woman. And he gave his message, as the council put it above, "in language intelligible to [his] generation." "Language" here involves not only his use of the local vernacular but also his style of presentation. He chose imagery, local references, and household and work allusions to present that message in ways that touched the imagination and the emotions. This style was absolutely essential because his message was not a theory but a way of life and a way of love. As John Henry Newman noted, "the heart is commonly reached, not through the reason, but through the imagination" (92).

One special example: he was Jesus of Nazareth, the apparent Bar-Joseph, yet his followers (and enemies) titled him *Messiah,* a culturally rich term for them, which was shifted into Greek as *Christ.* So our designation as *Christians* is itself part of an inculturation of the Good News of God's limitless love for us.

After Pentecost, the question arose: Who could be accepted into the assembly? While at Caesarea in the house of the centurion Cornelius, Peter had the first awareness that the group should be open to more than the people of Israel. "God has shown me that I should not call any person common or unclean. . . . Truly I perceive that God shows no partiality, but in every nation any one who fears him and does what is right is acceptable to him" (Acts 10:28, 34–35).

But the question for first-generation Apostles then became: Must one become Hebrew in order to become Christian? It became highlighted in the matter of ritual inculturation. Peter failed to be consistent to his insight received in Caesarea. The

fifteenth chapter of the Acts of the Apostles and the second
chapter of the Epistle to the Galatians deal with the first council
(in Jerusalem), working at whether the message of Jesus may be
separated from embodiment in Judaic culture and ritual. The
decision: one did not have to become Hebrew in order to become
Christian. Christianity could safely be opened to full embodiment in Graeco-Roman cultures.

What of cultural elements in moral rules that might be connected with the Gospel? In the Gospels themselves, Jesus consistently looks at all specific moral rules in the context of people
and evaluates whether they serve the people affected or not. His
moral concentration generally is on the behavior of those with
possessions and positions of power in society.

Paul, when writing of morals for Greeks, works with Stoic
virtues and vices; when writing for Romans, he employs the
Stoic natural law ethic. It is worthwhile noting that Stoic ethic
was originally embedded in a religious context other than Christian. So Paul provides an early example of an inculturation of
the Good News in the themes and images of a different religious
culture.

Some have found Paul's method of adopting non-Jewish ethics
to be an instructive aspect of inculturation in the matter of morality. Given such a process, it seems reasonable that the way
some moral standard may be expressed in Paul's epistles (for
example, regarding slavery or homosexuality or the subservi-
ence of women) need not settle a moral question for all time or
for all cultures. Karl Rahner, for one, thought it appropriate to
ask: "Must the marital morality of the Masai in East Africa simply reproduce the morality of the Christianity of Mediterranean
Europe? Or could a chieftain there, even if he is a Christian, live
in the style of the patriarch Abraham?" (79).

The context for Rahner's challenge comes with a tribal leader's
acceptance of Christian faith in Sub-Saharan Africa. In the nineteenth century, it was common for a tribal leader to have both
many wives and many slaves. The order from the Roman Curia
on the matter was given late in the nineteenth century: slavery is
not against natural law, so the leader may keep his slaves, but
polygamy is unnatural, so he must cast aside all but one wife. Of
course, in the culture, no other man would take in any woman so

cast out. Today, some African tribal leaders continue to have many wives.

Rahner, in this matter, does not deny objective moral values or general moral "laws." But he here offers a prudential judgment in which he seems to be like Thomas Aquinas, who, although respecting moral standards as needed to indicate moral attitudes, stated that universal "natural laws" often fail to settle what action or practice is called for in concrete contexts. For example, here the general value might be expressed as "respect the dignity of each person." But this respect needs the virtuous judgment in the context as to how best, given all the human values important in the context, to blend them all (Aristotle 1106b14–1107a2; Thomas Aquinas I-II, q. 94, art. 15).

Here we might also recall the answer Jesus gave to the question "Which is the greatest commandment?" "Love God with your whole heart, mind, and life; and the second, like unto this: Love your neighbor as yourself," the second of which he later amplified: "Love one another as I have loved you"—that is, giving my life for you.

I think here of the summary attributed to Rabbi Hillel: "What is hateful to you, do not to your neighbor; this is the entire Torah; all the rest is commentary" (483).

Some other examples in this first expression of inculturation of the Gospel might include early Christians taking over a *winter solstice* celebration from Latin religiousness and baptizing it Christmas, and taking over a northern European religious ceremony celebrating the Anglo-Saxon *goddess of spring* and baptizing it Easter. Neither of these celebrations would have made sense in Jerusalem.

But when Ambrose employed the Stoic theme of "goods of the earth meant for all humans" or Augustine used Platonic philosophic principles (such as that the physical world is not intelligible in itself, but only becomes so by forms given by Divine illumination), their transposing steps were not exactly examples of inculturation (although Ambrose's step was closer to inculturation than was Augustine's). Rather, they were "displacing" useful images from their original theoretical home.

Pieris gives an account as to how such a use of a "displaced" philosophy as an aid for theology became consciously welcomed. The metaphor of "philosophy as maidservant of theology" *(ancilla theologiae)* was given biblical authorization by Peter Damien's allegorical interpretation of a passage from the Hebrew Scriptures. In Deuteronomy 21:10–14, Yahweh gives permission for an Israelite to take a beautiful woman as a spouse out from among his captured enemies and keep her as long as she would be of service (Pieris 52). To consider images originating in the thought of another as items to be kept only as long as they are of service is not inculturation but rather exploitation. (Since the 1960s, the beautiful woman image has shifted from philosophy to psychology and sociology.)

At the close of the first millennium, when Roman officials organized into a Canon Law the many separate rules bishops had made over time, the Roman Church used the legal model in the earlier Roman Empire. This model included an office above the law that would be the final arbiter of disputes. It was only then that the Roman pope, at the time Gregory VII, became a juridical *sovereign.*

For most of the first one thousand years of the Church, there were five patriarchs who were thought of more as "servants of the servants" and who separately were in charge of the five *quite differently inculturated expressions* of the Gospel: Latin Rome, Egyptian Alexandria, Syrian Antioch, Byzantine Constantinople, and Jerusalem.

In the thirteenth century, Thomas Aquinas did his preparation at the University of Naples, where the study of the natural sciences of Aristotle was encouraged. At the time, Aristotle's philosophy was forbidden at most other European universities. Aquinas's later use of Aristotelian categories and, as Curtis Hancock notes in chapter 3 of this volume, of good elements in Jewish and Arab thinkers got him in continuous trouble during his teaching in Paris.

An engaging question: If Thomas, given his personality, were doing his studies today, what people would he be taking ideas from? Whom would he be reading most intently?

THE CHANGE IN ATTITUDE IN THE MODERN PERIOD

In the sixteenth and seventeenth centuries, the Roman Catholic Church lost its ability to inculturate both in the changing Europe and also in the newly entered lands of the New World and Asia. Perhaps this inability was owing to the breakup of European Christianity in the sixteenth and seventeenth centuries and to the Enlightenment's appeal to reason and self decision making in the eighteenth and nineteenth centuries.

The one major exception: the Council of Trent changed the ways of the officialdom of the Church into that of a modern political state and, viewing monarchy as the best form of government, led the way to a concept of the Church as a hierarchically ordered political power best headed by a sovereign monarch. But, whatever the cause of the loss of the ability to inculturate, the result was that official leaders from then on resisted allowing much to change the practices of the Church.

The first example of this resistance is central to our theme of inculturation. The official leaders appeared simply unimaginative in the matter of newly discovered lands and peoples. When some—for example, Roberto deNobili and Matteo Ricci—tried to introduce the Gospel in the lives of religious and cultural leaders in India and China (deNobili became a Hindu Brahman, Ricci a Chinese mandarin), the leaders rejected any possible symbiosis of ritual or way of expressing the Gospel with these Asian cultures. (A side comment: In those days, the Jesuit style was to influence a society's important and influential people in order to have the biggest and longest-lasting impact.)

In China, they specifically condemned religious ceremonies that honored ancestors! The only approved interchange was to find what in the other religion was compatible with Christianity as inculturated in Europe, not to find positive new ways and values in the other religions. As a result, the European understanding of the Gospel was scarcely altered.

Arnold Toynbee saw this venture in the East as the last real chance for the Catholic Church to become a truly world church, a truly catholic church—one, as Andrew Greeley phrases it, that means "here comes everybody" (9 and passim).

The second example of resistance concerned the changes within European culture itself. The leaders were quite ambiguous in the matter of the new sciences whenever these sciences touched on previous ways of expressing religious convictions. This ambiguity appears to be behind the ecclesiastical powers' burning Giordano Bruno at the stake in 1600 for proposing that the universe might be infinite and thus that the earth was not in the center of worlds numerous beyond counting.

But it was after the Enlightenment and the Age of Revolution that the Church leaders appeared to pull up every drawbridge. Even granted that there were many outspoken antireligious voices among the "liberals," the leaders failed to see any good in what was going on, especially in the areas of representative government, personal liberty, and the "social problem" of the new pattern of laborers in the Industrial Age.

Representative Government. After 1814, the papacy supported only restoration governments with hierarchical monarchies. There is some documentary and behavioral evidence to support that the Jesuits were called back from suppression to be central agents in this effort (Sheppard 100; Hollis 186–89, 219). Insofar as they did so, the restored Jesuits went contrary to their presuppression support for the authority of government coming not directly from God but from the people.

The insistence was still on the model of the Church that closely resembled a modern nation-state structured as a sovereign monarchy. Until Vatican II, much Catholic theology defended monarchy as the best governing structure.

Liberty. Gregory XVI in *Mirari Vos* characterized freedom of conscience as a "frenzy resulting from a diseased indifferentism" (14), even as it gained apace among some Catholic lay intellectuals (for example, Lamennais and Acton). The emphasis was that the Catholic Church possessed the "whole truth" with respect to our relationship with God and that, in some essential way, "outside the Church there is no salvation."

Labor Movements. In respect to the "social question" of the nineteenth century, until Leo XIII, official leaders could see only antihierarchy threats in urban labor movements.

Let us now return to today.

THE PRESENT AND SOME POSSIBILITIES

Karl Rahner saw as the theological significance of Vatican II that it stood forth as the first significant opening to a "World

Church," a Church that will be, in the literal meaning of the word, *catholic*. But for this opening to develop he believed it indispensable that we de-Europeanize the essentials of the Gospel. He found a historical analogy with the one previous great shift—from a Hebraic religious culture to a Graeco-Roman religious culture. Recall, the question then was: "Must one be Hebrew in order to become Christian?" How might he phrase the question today? Would it be something like this: "Must one be a southern-central European in order to become a disciple of the Good News?" Keep in mind, the name *Christian* itself is a title from Mediterranean cultures.

Yet the Vatican authorities in recent years have been continuously of two minds regarding any de-Europeanizing of the Gospel.

Responding to the Roman document *"Ecclesia* in Asia," the Asian bishops recently stressed the need for new ways to witness to the faith in a land where Catholics are 2 percent of the population. Their plan is to put less emphasis on speaking of the Good News in words and more on actual poverty and humble service. Asian bishops want to inculturate the liturgy to tie in with their effort to develop what they describe as a "dialogue with the cultures of Asia, dialogue with the religions of Asia, and with the peoples of Asia, especially the poor" (Special Synod 20).

In January 2000, the Vatican Curia refused the Asian bishops permission to develop the liturgy and liturgical texts in ways that the Asian bishops see as necessary for inculturation. The Asian bishops want to have Catholicism in Asia take on a more Asian face. They see the need for their churches increasingly to embody Asian values, such as stressing a deep sense of the Spirit and of harmony with all. Essentially, the Asian bishops want to give greater expression to a God who "unites and embraces all" (Ikenage 770) as we express "a Gospel that is embodied in our own lives" (Nomura 771). They are striving for an Asian image of Jesus, one sensitive to the ancient cultures and to the Asian deep sense of Spirit, using stories, images, symbols, parables, myths, and chanting of sacred texts.

Two examples from Carlos Valles may help here. One involves prayer. Most of us in the West experience prayer as involving words or recounting events, or at least in some way something happening, something from which, in Ignatius's phase, we can "draw some fruit." For many in Asia, however, the ideal is to empty consciousness completely. Valles proposes that this distinction is "the fundamental religious, theological, ascetical difference between East and West" (78).

A second example is the word *darshan*, which in India means "vision" and specifically a vision of God. One must be able to say, "Yes, I have seen God, and I can make you see him, too" in order to have authorization to speak about God. On this expectation of the devout Hindu to see God in this life, the Catholic monk Bede Griffiths comments, "Certainly in India we cannot expect the message of the Gospel to be accepted as a revelation from God if it offers less to the devout Hindu than his own religion" (Valles 97–98).

Of course, we do have such a religious experience in the Western tradition, but it is usually in the lives of ordinary people and remains unremarked by those writing prayer manuals. (Again, there are historical causes for such reluctance.)

There is the charming story of the working fellow who dropped into his church each afternoon after work. (In the days of the story, churches were open all day.) He would stay about half an hour. After a while, the pastor's curiosity could not be controlled, so one day he stopped the working fellow as he was leaving the church and asked him what he did in the church for half an hour. What prayers was he saying?

The worker, nonplussed, admitted he was saying no prayers.

The pastor, fearing the worst, then became more agitated. "Then what," he demanded, "do you do in there?"

The worker, now trembling, stuttered, "I don't do anything, Father. I just look at Jesus, and Jesus looks at me."

Of course, what the Asian bishops call for implies a *newly inculturated* Jesus, but what standard might guide us trying to inculturate the Good News of God today? May I suggest we might follow the first example? If the Second Person were to become incarnate to bring the Good News of God to people in Asia or in Africa today, what would this person look like, what local images and stories would this person use, what work analogies, in order to give a message "in language intelligible to each generation"?

In the capital of Mongolia has been started what might be the newest "parish" in the world. Its members are mostly young people, most of whom live in the city's sewers. How would the Second Person inculturate here?

A coworker with Gandhi, Kakasaheb Kalelkar, asked the Jesuit Carlos Valles, "If Jesus had been born in India, what concept of God would He have preached?" (Valles 59). We might expand that question and ask: What of Jesus incarnated in China? What of a Tahitian Jesus? A Navajo Jesus?

Let's reverse this line of query: How would you react to a Sri Lankan Jesus, a Hutu Jesus? We might compare this different Incarnation to what Asian and African peoples have had to react to for four hundred years.

In such inculturations, what would the Word have looked like? What parables and models would the Word have left us? Would the Word even have been a HE? Thomas Aquinas asked whether the Word, the Second Person of the Trinity, could have become incarnate many times (III, Q. 3, art. 7). For those who may find this idea difficult, let me just say that this medieval theologian, whom Leo XIII designated as a "safe" explainer of the faith, would not have been upset when he got to heaven to learn that the Second Person had done exactly that.

In the Hindu classic the *Bhagavadgita,* the Lord Shri Krishna's disciple Arjuna asks, interestingly, how Krishna could claim to have revealed something to someone who existed long before the present. Krishna responds: "I have been born again and again, at various times. . . . Whenever people live their lives without being mindful of their relation with God and materialism is unrestrained, then, O Arjuna, I reincarnate myself" (chapter 4, verses 5 and 7, my phrasing).

The Hindu author S. Radhakrishnan sees a connection here with the Gospel of John, 18:37: "Anyone committed to the Truth hears my voice" (152). This particular Gospel assertion must not be seen as if it were a tautology. If one must know and accept Jesus in order to live committed to the truth, then the statement is a triviality. So it must mean that whoever lives committed to the truth, even if such a one is not conscious of Jesus or does not believe in the Christian Gospel, nevertheless that one is hearing Jesus' voice.

And we might recall Peter's comment to the gathering at the home of Cornelius: "Truly I perceive that God shows no partiality, but in every nation any one who fears Him and does what is right is acceptable to Him" (Acts 10:34–35).

Clearly, our first task is to discern very carefully the Signs of the Times. And just as clearly, we cannot do spiritual discernment if the disposition is not right. However, amidst the post-Christian culture, it is quite obvious that many of us are fearful.

Here, John XXIII's words at the start of Vatican II are once again encouraging: "We feel we must disagree with these prophets of doom who are always forecasting disaster, as though the end of the world were at hand. . . . In the present order of things, Divine Providence is leading us to a new order of human relations which, by people's own efforts and even beyond their very expectations, are directed toward the fulfillment of God's superior and inscrutable designs" (426–27).

Likewise, as John Paul recently insisted in an encyclical devoted to the difficulty of evaluating contemporary systems of thought: *"discernment should not be seen as primarily negative"* (*Fides et Ratio*, 51, italics mine).

Let me end with a quote from Simone Weil, the French mystic who died in 1943 at the age of thirty-four. To the end, she refused to enter the Catholic Church precisely because of the leaders' attitude toward those who disagreed with its interpretation of God's action in other faiths. "Every time that anyone has, with a pure heart, called upon Osiris, Dionysus, Krishna, Buddha, the Tao, etc., the Son of God has answered that one by sending the Holy Spirit" (114).

WORKS CITED

Aquinas, Thomas. *Summa Theologiae.* Ottawa, Canada: Institute of Medieval Studies, 1941.

Aristotle. *Nicomachean Ethics.*

Dignitatis Humanae. December 7, 1965.

Gaudium et Spes. December 7, 1965.

Greeley, Andrew M. *The Communal Catholic.* New York: Seabury, 1977.

Gregory XVI. *Mirari Vos.* August 15, 1832.

Hillel. "The Elder." In *Encyclopedia Judaica Jerusalem*, vol. 8. Jerusalem: Keter, 1972.

Hollis, Christopher. *The Jesuits: A History.* New York: Macmillan, 1968.

Ikenage, Leo Jun. "Asian Ways of Expression." *Origins* 27 (May 7, 1998): 769–70.

John XXIII. "Speech Opening Vatican Council II, October 11, 1962." In *The Encyclicals and Other Messages of John XXIII*, 423–35. Washington, D.C.: TPS, 1964.

John Paul II. *Fides et Ratio.* September 14, 1998.

———. *Redemptoris Missio.* December 7, 1990.

Linden, Eugene. "The Exploding Cities of the Developing World." *Foreign Affairs* 75 (January–February 1996): 52–65.

Lumen Gentium. November 21, 1964.

Newman, John Henry. *The Grammar of Assent.* London: Longmans, Green, 1909.

Nomura, Augustinus Jun Ichi. "Communicating the Gospel in Japan." *Origins* 27 (May 7, 1998): 771.

Paul VI. *Evangelii Nuntiandi.* December 8, 1975.

Pieris, Aloysius. *An Asian Theology of Liberation.* Maryknoll, N.Y.: Orbis, 1988.

Pontifical Council for Culture. *Towards a Pastoral Approach to Culture.* Washington, D.C.: U.S. Catholic Conference, 1999.

Radhakrishnan, S. *The Bhagavadgita.* London: George Allen and Unwin, 1948.

Rahner, Karl. "Basic Theological Interpretation of the Second Vatican Council," and "The Abiding Significance of the Second Vatican Council: Concern for the Church." In *Theological Investigations XX*, 77–89 and 90–102. New York: Crossroad, 1981.

Sheppard, Lancelot. *Lacordiare.* London: Burns and Oates, 1964.

Special Synod of Asia. "Message to the People of God." *Origins* 28 (May 28, 1998): 17–22.

Valles, Carlos. *Sketches of God.* Chicago: Loyola University Press, 1987.

Weil, Simone. *Gateway to God.* London: Collins Fontana, 1974.

6

Pastoral Sociology at the Millennium: Challenges and Opportunities

Robert J. Mahoney

WHAT IS PASTORAL SOCIOLOGY, and what has it to do with pastoral care? What, if anything, can pastoral sociology tell us about the future of the Catholic Church in the United States? Is this something new? I address those questions and more. First, let's *do* some pastoral sociology.

A brief study of the general summary of *The Official Catholic Directory* (2151) provokes some serious pastoral reflections. From 1988 to 1998, the total number of priests serving in U.S. dioceses has shrunk from 58,522 to 47,563. At the same time, the total number of Catholics in the United States has risen from 53,496,862 to 61,563,769. *In other words, during the past decade, the number of priests in U.S. dioceses has declined by an average of about 1,100 a year, whereas the number of their Catholic flocks has increased by an average of well more than 800,000 a year!*

These basic figures are not the whole story. Remaining priests are predominantly older. Priestly decline will continue and increase as these older priests die and retire. Replacement priests in needed numbers are not on the horizon. Vocations may be rising in some parts of the world, but not in the United States. The number of diocesan seminarians has declined from 4,981 in 1988 to 3,248 in 1998. If we were to *triple* the number of seminarians presently in diocesan seminaries and ordain all of them next week, we would barely match the decline of priests during the past decade and do little or nothing to deal with the expanding number of Catholics needing priests. These recent figures are fairly startling. Yet similar demographics of the priest shortage have been documented and forecast for years (Schoenherr and Young; Schoenherr and Sorenson).

Pastoral sociologists study this kind of trend and other pastoral matters in order to uncover pastoral realities and plumb causes and consequences, the kind of information essential for informed response to pastoral needs. We also study the official Church's response—or lack of response—to pastoral challenges. (From now on, when I use the word *Church* with a capital "C," I am referring to the Roman Catholic Church.)

Catholic pastors are responsible for all of the souls assigned to their care. Bishops have the responsibility of orchestrating priorities and patterns of pastoral care for entire jurisdictions, usually dioceses. The Episcopal conference or hierarchy of a country has these responsibilities as well as the challenge of assessing and addressing the spiritual needs of a total society; and the hierarchy of each society looks to Rome for ultimate authority. It seems reasonable that pastors at all levels in the Church would desire the most accurate information possible about the state of the souls in their care. Yet, as we shall see, this is not always the case.

We have good news and bad news. The good news is that American Catholics have access to the best tools for pastoral need assessment and planning in the entire history of the Church. The bad news is that for too many pastors at all ranks, these tools remain unknown, woefully underutilized, widely misunderstood, or all of the above.

This chapter briefly explains pastoral sociology, examines its history and pioneers, and gives several examples of the consequences of its use and abuse, including excerpts from a parish study I conducted. I then list a few of many "red flag" pastoral issues confronting American Catholics at the portals of the new millennium.

First, however, consider two mythic statements about pastoral research: (1) "Let's not get excited; Christ promised that the Catholic Church is going to survive to the end of the world, regardless"; and (2) "The Church is guided by the Holy Spirit, and the old ways are good enough."

Like all myths, these statements are a mixture of truth, fiction, and poetry. Overburdened pastors juggle heavy routine demands with unexpected needs and emergencies. Pastors today easily can miss contact with parishioners who avoid them yet need pastoral attention. Parish priests can't do their job alone; happily, powerful help is available under the general heading of "pastoral sociology."

As a priest, I believe that the Church will survive till the end of the world in some manner, whether flourishing or as a "saving remnant." History, however, teaches us that in any given society or age the Church can undergo grave setbacks and virtually vanish in that time and place. The history of the Catholic Church is spotted with such instances. The American Catholic Church is not immune.

As a sociologist, I believe that pastoral sociology offers great potential for assessing needs of the faithful—and the proper responses—at all levels of church operation. History teaches us that complacency is not an acceptable pastoral option.

As we begin the third millennium, the American Catholic Church is at a crossroad. Great opportunities exist for better care of souls. Yet it is possible that unless we honestly and efficiently investigate and address key pastoral needs, the Catholic Church in the United States may face crises even while the Catholic Church in some other cultures may be exploding with vitality.

PASTORAL SOCIOLOGY

Sociologists study what happens when people interact—all the way from a "dyad," or two persons, to groups small and large, including organizations, institutions, and even whole societies and cultures. Sociology is an empirical science, meaning that its methods include careful, precise, and objective observations and measurements.

There are limitations. Sociological methodology admits of some practical imprecision. Human beings are complex and mysterious, influenced by hidden and subtle forces both internal and external. Also, we sociologists are human and have biases, which may influence the way we interpret what we observe. Further, sociologists generally are guided by theoretical positions

whose assumptions also may influence choice of topic and interpretation of data. The nature of sociological theories and the
origins of the discipline have made many critics—especially religious critics—wary of using sociology and sometimes strongly
prejudiced against it.

Even when sociology *is* practiced most effectively and objectively, it may generate the fiercest opposition if its findings challenge conventional wisdom. Pastoral sociology is particularly
prone to controversy because it applies its scientific methods to
find out what is actually happening at ground zero in religion,
an area of great passion and conviction. The traditional tensions
between religion and sociology aggravate this controversy. Let's
explore why.

Sociology emerged as a science in eighteenth-century and especially nineteenth-century European intellectual circles in the
wake of the Reformation and the Enlightenment, and as the age
of modern science dawned. Many intellectuals became dis-
gusted with the religious struggles and social chaos following
the Reformation. Intoxicated by the rationalism of the Enlightenment and galvanized by the triumphs of the "objective" methodology of nineteenth- and twentieth-century natural science,
scholars blended both to craft sociology as the new science of
society.

The Reformation shattered religious unity. The nineteenth
century saw scientific advances question the origin and meaning
of the universe. In like manner, the new science of society—
sociology—not only questioned religion, but also threatened to
replace it. By definition, early sociologists tended to be liberal
and frequently skeptical, agnostic, or atheistic.

In general, sociological theories view society and morality as
human inventions or adaptations. A sociological functionalist
may explain religion as a pragmatic invention—or borrowed cultural convention—for promoting social solidarity, reinforcing
social norms, and coping with life's fears, mysteries, and trage-
dies. A Marxist sees religion as a tool capitalists use to quell
dissent among the poor and exploit them by inducing the poor
to "offer up" their sad lot rather than rebel and fight for reform.

Religionists reacted with alarm and defensiveness. In return, scientists were suspicious of religion's perceived tendency to censor and suppress the legitimate pursuit of truth. We might call this the "Galileo Effect."

By the mid–twentieth century, sociology was well entrenched in higher education. However, in Catholic colleges and universities in the first half of the twentieth century, sociology frequently differed greatly from its counterpart on secular campuses. "Catholic" sociology courses sometimes were really about social justice and included a heavy dose of papal encyclicals. Secular universities and "mainstream sociology" emphasized objectivity and methodology and a variety of guiding theoretical perspectives. Sociologists' view of religion ranged from disinterest to curiosity to coolness to hostility.

Under these circumstances, it is understandable that sociology did not come immediately to mind when the Church needed to address pastoral questions.

This situation began to change in the 1940s and thereafter, as more Catholics and Catholic clerics here and abroad began to seek graduate degrees in sociology from highly respected secular universities. A number of these Catholic scholars realized the potential for pastoral assessment and planning inherent in the methodology of sociology. About mid–twentieth century, pastoral sociology began to be explored. Although much progress has been made, fifty years later pastoral sociology remains both one of our most potent and most neglected tools for effective pastoral care.

In the mid-1960s, *Sociology and Pastoral Care* by François Houtart was translated from the French *Sociologie et pastorale.* Houtart, a priest born in Brussels who studied at the University of Chicago and taught at the University of Louvain, argued that pastoral sociology was as important as pastoral theology in today's complex care of souls. In the introduction to Houtart's small book, Cardinal Suenens argues that the "role of human sciences makes them the auxiliaries of . . . [pastoral] . . . care." The cardinal hopes that "the bridge may be more and more solidly established between the sociologists and the pastors" (Houtart vi). In the next section, I examine the beginning of that partnership in the United States.

A Brief Historical Sketch of Pastoral Sociology

As noted earlier, although sociology arose as a discipline in the nineteenth century, it wasn't until the mid–twentieth century that collaboration between sociology and pastoral care would begin to overcome considerable ignorance and bias on both sides. Two pioneers of pastoral sociology illustrate both the promise and the peril of their "new" subfield: Father Joseph Fichter, S.J., a Jesuit priest, and Father Andrew Greeley, a diocesan priest, both with excellent sociological credentials.

Fichter undertook a study of a southern urban parish—a massive study of pastoral circumstances planned for publication in four volumes under the series title *Southern Parish*. The University of Chicago Press published volume 1, *Dynamics of a City Church*, in 1951. Following practice of the day, the Jesuit Fichter obtained required ecclesiastical as well as editorial approval for the multivolume publication of results from his lengthy and exhaustive study. A number of critics, including some very prominent sociological scholars, acclaimed the first volume as a major accomplishment.

Today, we may not be surprised that Fichter found his target parish peopled with less than perfect parishioners. It *did* surprise the pastor of the parish, who was shocked to learn that unsuspected numbers of his parishioners often or regularly missed mass, received the sacraments sporadically if at all, and married or lived together without benefit of clergy—along with other depressing news.

Instead of gladly using Fichter's data to address pastoral needs, the chagrined pastor reacted angrily. He eventually prevailed on ecclesiastical authorities, including Fichter's Jesuit Provincial, to suppress the remaining three volumes of the series. Fichter went on to other studies, which *were* published, and to a distinguished sociological career. Many years later, he gave a detailed and balanced account of the virulent attacks on his first study and its suppression (Fichter, *One-Man Research*, 28–75).

Fichter's experience still echoes today. His study was among the first scientific empirical studies to determine the actual practices of Catholics in a parish and to ask what level of participation might be "normal." It became evident that many ill-informed pastors might resent *any* data that questioned their pastoral awareness. In truth, pastors had no real "benchmark" studies with which to compare an accurate analysis of their own parishes. Without a benchmark, what appeared to be "bad" news might really be well within the "normal" range, even if less than ideal. A national study to set such a benchmark was years away (Castelli and Gremillion).

In the 1950s, "good" parishes were those with full churches on Sunday, enjoying plentiful participation in the sacraments, especially baptism, confession (Penance), communion (Eucharist), and marriage. Pastors (and parishioners) also judged parish success by substantial income (regular and special collections), levels of debt and pace of debt reduction, numbers of "registered" parishioners, and size of the physical plant. Other criteria included a solid nucleus of "good" families, a full complement of active parish organizations (Altar Society, Holy Name Society, Legion of Mary, Catholic Scout Troops, and so on), and preferably a school with religious sisters or brothers as teachers, supported by a strong PTA.

Some criteria were clearly quantitative—for example, amounts of cash flow, parish indebtedness, the quantity of communion hosts consumed, baptisms administered, and so on— but many were *qualitative perceptions* by pastor and people. Although "good" pastors knew many parishioners by name or by sight, studies such as Fichter's called into question the status and active participation of significant numbers of parishioners, which could threaten an insecure pastor and challenge the extent and accuracy of his pastoral awareness in the absence of valid, objective data (Fichter, *One-Man Research*, 28–75).

The competent pastor needs much more than superficial quantification and "intuitive" perceptions, and not all in-depth findings will be positive. *Nevertheless, valid findings—positive or negative—are urgently needed for informed, effective pastoral care.*

Even today, some pastors react to parish study negatives— scope of *non*participation, levels of faith defection, invalid marriages, premarital sex, birth control, abortion—with denial or by "shooting the messenger," as happened with Fichter's first study; others welcome hard data that can highlight pastoral needs and help prioritize pastoral efforts. *After all, how can we* *serve pastoral needs unless we know them or understand their degrees of urgency?*

In the years following Fichter's study, an expanding circle of pastors has slowly come to realize that the size of their parishes and the routine duties that filled their days often led to a deceptively narrow tunnel vision of the souls in their care. Unfortunately, many more pastors have *not* come to this realization, even as the priest shortage and drought in vocations intensified throughout the 1990s, severely limiting the ability of ever fewer pastors to know ever-expanding numbers of faithful.

A second priest sociologist with a stormier personality conducted much pastoral research and stirred frequent debate. Father Andrew Greeley, a priest of the Chicago archdiocese and a tireless researcher and writer for almost forty years, challenged many preconceptions and stereotypical ideas about the Catholic Church. A bibliography of Greeley's hundreds of books and articles fills a very large volume. For years, he wrote a widely syndicated column that was read by "ordinary" Catholics as well as by Church leaders. For some time now, he has enjoyed great commercial success with a series of "Catholic" novels, in addition to continuing his scholarly work.

Greeley has a legion of critics and admirers both within and outside the Catholic Church. Critics dismiss his work because of its sheer volume—"never had an unpublished thought"; because his work is too Catholic or not Catholic enough; because he is at times outspokenly emotional, polemical, and "thin-skinned"; because his conclusions are stated as absolutes; because he is a "popularizer"; because he is too liberal or not liberal enough. Admirers see Greeley as a Don Quixote with data, tilting at ecclesiastical and sociological windmills, drawing attention to urgent pastoral needs, a professional's professional, a skilled researcher and scholar, a stimulating gladiator for a vital Church, a man in the tradition of "doctors of the Church," and a man most unlikely to be given that rare title because of the controversies—and enmities—he has provoked.

Fans describe him as warm, caring, charming, and witty, and as a loyal friend, a fine priest, a brilliant intellect, and a great scholar; foes see him as arrogant, opinionated, angry, sarcastic, irreverent, prickly, and stubborn. Greeley has not suffered fools—or critics—gladly, and his more memorable disagreements with authorities and colleagues, both secular and religious, have been fierce, acrimonious, and sometimes very public.

The real Greeley probably exists somewhere in a mix of very different and often contradictory perceptions of him. The fact is, however, that whether we like him or not, agree with him or not, for decades he has striven to hew a powerful sociological understanding of the Catholic faith and its pastoral needs.

In the fall of 1999, an instructive event occurred. A panel at the annual meeting of the American Sociological Association, held that year in Chicago, gave Greeley's work a retrospective review. A panel of scholars addressed his body of work with appreciation, occasional good-natured gibes, and great respect. Greeley, for his part, didn't talk about himself but simply presented some interesting research findings concerning Russian religion today.

Cardinal George of Chicago was in the audience, a few rows from where I was sitting. Afterward, Greeley came down to greet the cardinal and said, "You are the first bishop to attend one of my presentations." If accurate, it was an instructive and poignant comment on the hierarchy's reaction—or lack of reaction—to his remarkable body of pastoral and sociological work extending over nearly four decades and countless rebuffs.

A decade before this incident, in an article titled "Sociology and the Catholic Church: Four Decades of Bitter Memories," Greeley had written a very pessimistic assessment of the Church leadership's exclusion of pastoral sociology from serious consideration.

As I wrote these words in June 2000, a study on the priest shortage, originating from the Center for Applied Research in the Apostolate (CARA), not as yet released for general publication, was being presented in Milwaukee to the meeting of the National Conference of Catholic Bishops and was reported nationwide in several stories by CNN television and CNN.com on June 16 and June 18.

Among the grim statistics covered in the study: more than 2,300 parishes without resident priests, a dramatic drop in the total number of priests, an equally dramatic rise in the number of parishioners, an aging clergy, and a declining seminary enrollment. An auxiliary bishop told of megaparishes in the Los Angeles archdiocese with as many as *18,000 households!* The number of immigrants in some of these megaparishes has swelled, adding great complexities of language, legal status, gang culture, and poverty to the pastoral challenge.

Certainly this is a story of national religious crisis, but it is hardly news! The figures on this very problem, given at the beginning of this chapter, are from *The Official Catholic Directory* of 1998. Schoenherr and Young published a book on the problem— *Full Pews and Empty Altars: Demographics of the Priest Shortage in United States Catholic Dioceses*—in 1993. Wallace wrote of the increasing use of women as parish administrators in 1992. Schoenherr and Sorensen wrote about consequences of declining clergy numbers in 1982.

Almost twenty years of pastoral research detailing and projecting the decline in the number of U.S. priests has prompted very little *effective* response from the Church. Pastoral sociologists must wonder at what point in this mounting crisis will *decades* of pastoral research projections and warnings finally receive serious attention.

Has the Church, then, totally ignored pastoral sociology and the insights that it provides for the effective care of souls?

Not totally. Fichter discerned a "great awakening to the need of sociological research" among American Catholic bishops in the wake of the Second Vatican Council, but charitably didn't belabor the fact that this "great awakening" came almost two decades after his own pioneering work (*One-Man Research* 7). Fichter's evidence of this awakening was the $50,000 that the bishops spent on a study of seminarians (Potvin) and their subsequent employment of the National Opinion Research Center to conduct a $440,000 study of the American priesthood.

Fichter notes that his own research studies have been much more modest in cost and scope, in part because of his university teaching responsibilities and in part because pastors and bishops were reluctant to pay for serious professional research and definitely did not want it published (*One-Man Research* 6–8).

Fichter, Greeley, and other pastoral sociology pioneers eventually had company. An outstanding example is the previously noted Center for Applied Research in the Apostolate (CARA), officially incorporated in the District of Columbia on August 4, 1964. In 1951, as Fichter was discovering the realpolitik of Church research, a call was being made by the superiors of missionary institutes for a national research center. Richard Cardinal Cushing took up the call for such a center to assist missionaries in 1961 and saw it a reality about three years later. Cushing was CARA's honorary first president. Fathers Fichter and Greeley were members of the CARA Research Council in 1966. Fichter would later write that although they met periodically, the council—or "committee" as he describes it—had "no clear idea of its duties" and no financial support from the bishops (*One Man Research* 13). CARA sought funds on its own from various sources.

Archbishop (later Cardinal) John Patrick Cody was chairman of the CARA board of directors from 1964 to 1966. Ironically, and unfortunately, years later there would be a bitter and widely publicized break between Cardinal Cody, then archbishop of Chicago, and his best-known Chicago priest-sociologist, Father Andrew Greeley. Still later, Greeley would experience coolness and some estrangement from another archbishop of Chicago, Cardinal Bernardin.

Personality and professional clashes such as these, as well as lack of interest, understanding, and funding, sometimes did mar and impede the work of pastoral sociology. Even so, CARA moved steadily into studies of the priesthood and vocations, pastoral planning, and the "management and administration of dioceses, parishes, and religious communities" (Center for Applied Research in the Apostolate 10). The CARA Renew Program claims to have reached some four million Catholics in 130 U.S. dioceses (although this number is but a fraction of American Catholic population). In addition, there has been work on campus ministries, aging religious orders, evangelization, disaffection of Hispanics and other recent immigrant groups, the home missions, urban religious problems, Catholic health ministry, and a variety of other pastoral issues.

At Georgetown University, CARA has produced many publications on these pastoral topics and others during its thirty-six years of operation. Additional organizations under varied sponsorship, such as the Notre Dame Institute for Pastoral and Social Ministry, also have contributed to pastoral research.

The Conference for Pastoral Planning and Council Development (CPPCD) is located in St. Louis, Missouri. Sister M. Frances Schumer, A.S.C., the CPPCD executive director, informs me that persons taking their Certificate Program in Pastoral Planning have expressed need for more help with pastoral research and that the CPPCD is responding. Sister Fran's group has a particular interest in social relations in parish councils, an area where many pastors and parishioner-council members struggle to find a formula for successful cooperation. (Both CARA and the CPPCD have web sites: visit www.georgetown.edu/research/cara/index.html and www.cppcd.org for further information.)

Some dioceses have sufficient size and resources to have fairly elaborate research centers "in-house." An example is the New York Archdiocesan Office of Pastoral Research and Planning. In October 1999, its director, Dr. Ruth T. Doyle, received the Father Louis Luzbetak, S.V.D., Award for Exemplary Church Research from CARA. Father Luzbetak was executive director of CARA in its first decade; now eighty-one and retired, he was present for the presentation to Doyle of the CARA award named for him.

Dr. Doyle tells me that both efforts at in-house and interdenominational research projects are being explored in New York. Among many types of pastoral research data, Doyle finds U.S. Census and other demographic reports useful for profiling pastoral vicariates. She reports that realistic age profiling is an example of data use that can impact pastoral care.

Doyle mentions one New York parish in which the median age of its parishioners was thought to be in the fifties or sixties, but research found the actual median age to be twenty-nine, which led to restructured parish services, including the development of a preschool program and other forms of outreach. In another instance, a "fading" parish in a theater district perceived to be heavily transient was discovered to have a significant and stable elder population. Directing services to that previously "invisible" elder parish population reinvigorated the parish. Dr. Doyle's office also helps develop data for the evaluation of pastors, with the cooperation of the pastors and selected parishioners.

Following in Fichter's, Greeley's, and pastoral research organizations' wake has been a heartening growth in the number of individuals, programs, and resources related to pastoral care. Several organizations devoted to sociology of religion—the Religious Research Association, the Society for the Scientific Study of Religion, and the Association for the Sociology of Religion—provide publishing and paper presentation opportunities for researchers, which helps stimulate pastoral scholarship.

Two of Greeley's many books are of particular interest to those dipping into pastoral research. *Religious Change in America* summarizes a great amount of religious research data in a concise and readable manner. Given the brief life span of most books today, it may be significant that I recently purchased a copy of the 1996 edition of the book off the shelf at a Borders bookstore, now in its third printing a decade after its first publication. Another interesting (*Newsday* called it "engrossing") book by Greeley is *The Catholic Myth: The Behavior and Beliefs of American Catholics*, which covers a wide spectrum of Catholic pastoral interests.

Greeley is correct that sufficient funding is lacking and research design can be tricky; nevertheless, he insists that more research on priest–people relationships is needed and could be of immense value not only for pastors but also for the training of future priests. Parish-related sociological research and writing are growing (Dolan; Sweetser and Holden; Sweetser and McKinney; Wallace). Hands-on pastoral experience—at least as an adjunct source of pastoral information—is producing material for more general spiritual use (Brennan; Wicks and Rodgerson).

Research of individual parishes, such as the personal example I give later in this essay, cannot be generalized to all or even most parishes, but such research does help suggest potentially rewarding lines of inquiry for larger studies and *can* help the individual parish very importantly, with tailor-made information.

Pastoral research need not focus on the individual parish to be helpful. Broader research about American Catholics provides evidence about the Catholic population as a whole and about its relationship to the American culture. This research serves as a partial corrective to both "intellectual" and street-level bigotry that views the Roman Catholic Church as "foreign," "un-American," or "anti-intellectual." Incidentally, these works also help Catholics see themselves as distinctly American and less ghettoized (Massa; Rigney and Hoffman; Wakin and Scheuer; Yuhaus).

Another example of this overall view is *Catholicism USA: A Portrait of the Catholic Church in the United States,* a CARA project edited by Bryan T. Froehle and Mary L. Gautier, and published in the summer of 2000, which brings together a great deal of research information.

Early works in this vein gave a sense of embattlement. In his 1976 book *The Communal Catholic,* Andrew Greeley sharply challenges positions both within and outside the Church, and he makes it clear that this aggressive posture was intentional: "This book is written with every deliberate intention to make trouble" (vii). Greeley sees future Church leadership as coming "neither from the official hierarchy nor from the self-appointed quasi-official intelligentsia" (ix). Greeley's later work, although always feisty, is gradually more mature and balanced.

The Catholic Research Forum, most of whose members participate in the CPPCD, may be accessed on the Internet at http://www.execpc.com/~mcieslak/crf/mission.htm, where it succinctly states its mission: "The Catholic Research Forum's purpose is to share the results of applied empirical research about the Catholic Church with people who can use the research fruitfully in their ministries. The Forum dialogs regularly with the U.S. Bishops' Conference, individual bishops, canon lawyers, pastoral planners, and others who are in leadership positions in dioceses or parishes" (Catholic Research Forum).

Also, Brother John Raymond has compiled a very stimulating and useful book, *Catholics on the Internet: 2000–2001,* listing more than 10,000 Catholic sites in 280 categories.

Diocesan web pages are quite common, although they vary widely in quality and usage. Because communication about the faith, including instruction and evangelization, goes to the core of what the Church is about, pastoral researchers will need to keep the Internet in mind as a tool in this new millennium. The National Conference of Catholic Bishops, United States Catholic

Conference, has scheduled a small publication on the Internet, *Your Family and Cyberspace*. However, much like the business world, the Church is only beginning to determine how to harness the Internet.

An Example of Pastoral Sociology Research

I now turn to a very specific example of pastoral research. In 1991–92, I researched a suburban, largely blue-collar parish at the request of the pastor and Parish Ministry Council and consulted with them through part of 1993.

The pastor and Parish Ministry Council of a somewhat troubled parish sought to unearth the real state of the parish, determine its pastoral needs, and initiate a new beginning. More than eight hundred parishioners responded to a lengthy questionnaire. In retrospect, two questions proved to be especially instructive (Mahoney, "Pluralism or Polarity").

First, I asked the parishioners their reaction to the "Parish Mission Statement" that their pastor had crafted. More than half of the respondents (60.4 percent) either had not heard of the mission statement or were unclear how it might affect them. *An unknown and unclear mission statement is not helpful.*

Second, I asked the respondents to rank nine possible pastoral priorities in order of importance. The same question was asked of the pastor, the Parish Ministry Council, and the parish staff. Tables 1–4 give the responses (Mahoney, "Pluralism or Polarity," 22–23), and my comments are based on the questionnaire and on my meetings and consultations with the pastor and Parish Ministry Council and the parish staff over a period of months (eventually there also were two open meetings for the parish as a whole).

The tables make clear how sometimes relatively simple questions can open new lines of communication and discussion when there is good will *and* good data. 1. *There was a clear disjuncture between parish leadership and the parish community in the ranking of pastoral priorities.* Theologically and pastorally, the pastor and Parish Ministry Council and parish staff priority given to the Eucharist was both legitimate and appropriate.

Table 1: Pastoral Priorities, Parishioners

Most Important	1. Care of the sick
	2. Ministry to the aged
	3. Youth ministry
	4. Social services, support groups
	5. Rich liturgical/sacramental life
	6. Seminars on sexual ethics, problems, AIDS
	7. Adult religious education
	8. Parish prayer group
Least Important	9. Old-time mission

Archbishop Oscar H. Lipscomb of Mobile, Alabama, and chairman of the U.S. bishops' Committee on the Liturgy, said it well in a March 2000 address: "The Eucharist—the body and blood of Christ really, truly and substantially present—plays an irreplaceable role in the quality and perseverance of people's faith" (qtd. in Sly 1).

The pastor enjoyed the liturgy and seemed to pride himself on a liturgically rich mass. He seemed surprised that only a little more than half (56.5 percent) found the liturgy as a whole generally satisfactory.

It was clear that the parishioners saw things differently, yet not unreasonably. They may have taken for granted the centrality of the Eucharist and may have addressed priorities in terms of perceived pastoral weakness. A second possibility is that in spite of the careful liturgical planning, its execution was not

Table 2: Parishioner Priority Response by Age and Gender (Female)

Female 45 or younger	Female 46 or older
1. Care of the sick	1. Care of the sick
2. Ministry to the aged	2. Ministry to the aged
3. Social services, support groups	3. Youth ministry
4. Youth ministry	4. Rich liturgical/sacramental life
5. Rich liturgical/sacramental life	5. Social services, support groups
6. Seminars on sexual ethics	6. Adult religious education
7. Adult religious education	7. Seminars on sexual ethics
8. Old-time mission	8. Parish prayer group
9. Parish prayer group	9. Old-time mission

Table 3: Parishioner Response by Age and Gender (Male)

Male 45 or younger	*Male 46 or older*
1. Care of the sick	1. Care of the sick
2. Seminars on sexual ethics	2. Ministry to the aged
3. Social services, support groups	3. Rich liturgical/sacramental life
4. Youth ministry	4. Youth ministry
5. Rich liturgical/sacramental life	5. Social services, support groups
6. Ministry to the aged	6. Adult religious education
7. Adult religious education	7. Seminars on sexual ethics
8. Parish prayer group	8. Parish prayer group
9. Old-time mission	9. Old-time mission

fully successful in stressing the centrality of the Eucharist and its importance in the spiritual lives of parishioners. A third possibility is sociological. The pastor in an earlier parish assignment had developed a liturgical style that apparently evoked a warm response. The present parish was different in socioeconomic, age, and racial-ethnic dimensions. These kinds of differences may require important adjustments to accomplish the best liturgical configuration for a particular parish.

2. *The emphasis on visiting the sick seemed to take the pastor, Parish Council, and staff somewhat by surprise.* There were several factors here. The pastor was of a relatively young cohort of priests at the forefront of changed dynamics in the post–Vatican II Church, which have been described as moving the priest from

Table 4: Pastoral Priorities by Parish Staff, Pastor/Parish Ministry Council

Parish Staff	*Pastor/Parish Ministry Council*
1. Rich liturgical/sacramental life	1. Rich liturgical/sacramental life
2. Social services, support groups	2. Youth ministry
3. Adult religious education	3. Adult religious education
4. Care of the sick	4. Social services, support groups
5. Ministry to the aged	5. Ministry to the aged
6. Youth ministry	6. Care of the sick
7. Parish prayer group	7. Seminars on sexual ethics
8. Seminars on sexual ethics	8. Parish prayer group
9. Old-time mission	9. Old-time mission

ombudsman and father figure to "orchestra leader" (Dolan et al. 89–107). A number of scholars have reflected on the generational changes among American priests in the twentieth century (Hoge, Shields, and Verdieck; Verdieck, Shields, and Hoge; Young et al.; Hoge, Shields, and Griffin).

This middle generation of priests tends to see their work as ranging from liturgical presiding to bureaucratic managing to collaboration with Parish Councils and people. Thomas Sweetser, S.J., and Carol M. Holden have written of the new priest "facilitator" and of the shift of emphasis to the community. These writers and others warn the priest against trying to do too much. In many instances, the priest has evolved into a manager, and a business model may emerge, complete with workday office hours, a separation of residence, and especially a delegation of tasks. This configuration involves an almost inevitable distancing of priest from parishioner.

3. *The pastor seemed to see the desire of the people for constant accessibility as unrealistic, if not impossible.* Many of the people in the parish were older than the pastor, and the older profile of the parishioners may have had two effects: (1) many members of an age familiar with (and perhaps nostalgic for) the older style of pastoral service; and (2) many parishioners having intimations of mortality and concerned about what will happen to them or their loved ones when they face death. In response to a related question, 77.7 percent either agreed or strongly agreed that it was "of primary concern that a priest be available or at least accessible for emergency calls at all times, even if special equipment or services might be required" (Mahoney, "Pluralism or Polarity," 26).

The escalating demands can grind down and burn out priests. There is no simple answer. Dialog between pastor and parishioners can help educate both as to the desirable versus the possible with regard to pastoral availability as well as the best use of limited time and energy.

4. *Prior to the study, there appeared to be a major morale problem in the parish, especially related to perception and attitude.* Parish Ministry Council members and others had indicated that they thought the parish was "cold," "unfriendly," "cliquish," and "unwelcoming." Supposedly, parishioners were defecting,

"abandoning ship." A positive finding of the study was that seven out of ten parishioners (71.5 percent) actually viewed the parish as warm, friendly, and caring.

It seems that council members and some parishioners did not quite grasp the demographics: older parishioners were dying or going to nursing care, not abandoning the parish; there were fewer younger parishioners, and these younger people were fairly likely to move for reasons unrelated to the parish (jobs, education, etc.).

5. *The problem of sexual instruction disturbed some parishioners and Parish Ministry Council members.* There is an epidemic of premarital sex; AIDS continues to spread; and sexually transmitted diseases are a major medical scourge. Yet there are also spiritual consequences to sexual behavior and misbehavior. We are living in a culture saturated with sex on television, in the movies, in magazines, in advertising. For example, the top-rated, award-winning, well-written, and superbly acted situation comedy *Frasier* constantly and wittily presents casual and serial sexual promiscuity as perfectly normal and expected—without even a hint of any significant negative consequences for that behavior. Cable offers *Sex and the City*, *Real Sex*, and MTV. Pardun and McKee found religious images were more likely than not to accompany sexual imagery—possibly to legitimize its use?

Although reliable sex research shows an encouraging (and perhaps surprising) respect for marriage vows among Americans (Laumann et al.), attitudes about premarital sex are a different story. Catholics appear to be affected by this cultural acceptance of free and easy sex, particularly premarital sex (Petersen and Donnenwerth; Cochran and Beeghley). My parish study responses from teenagers are instructive:

> Keeping in mind the enormously powerful role of peers in socialization, it is worth noting that 91.6 percent of the responding teens agreed that today, "regardless of religious affiliation, most young people will engage in sexual relations before marriage," and 83.1 percent agree that the majority of teenagers will experience their first sexual relations before leaving high school. Further, half (51.7 percent) do NOT FEEL THAT Catholic teenagers are less likely to engage in premarital sex than are non-Catholic teens (Mahoney, "Working Paper #8," 6).

More than a third of the teenage respondents felt it was "not wrong at all" for a man and a woman to have sexual relations before marriage. The teenagers were a small subsample of the parish study, and we can't generalize to a larger population, but the answers were consistent and provocative.

McNamara has noted a decline in Catholic religious beliefs and practices in the mid-1960s, which continued in the 1970s, and he looks to personal morality issues as signs of religious decline. He points especially to issues such as birth control, divorce with remarriage, and premarital sex.

In my 1991–92 study, young male adults listed instruction in sex ethics as their second highest priority, but the Parish Ministry Council seemed reluctant to address the matter of sex instruction. The pastor appeared more willing to respond. However, given the complex sexual scene in the United States today, pastors in general may not be adequately prepared for this task.

Six "Red Flag" Areas of Pastoral Sociology Concern

As we American Catholics enter the third millennium of Christianity, research, policy, and action need to address some sobering challenges. Here are a few of those "pastoral red flags" of the new millennium.

The Need for Professional Research Assistance

Research appears simple. It is not. The crafting of questions is challenging even for professionals. Amateur research can be misleading and counterproductive. Pastors need to seek and fund professional research, welcome and use results, and encourage publication. Anonymous surveys should complement focus groups and other "open" group inquiries, which may inhibit expression of certain "uncomfortable" questions and opinions and restrict or manipulate outcomes.

Socialization of the Faithful

We have pride and a *huge* vested interest in our Catholic schools and in the Rite of Christian Initiation for Adults (RCIA). Still, when we examine Catholic parishioners—including school children and teens, young and old adults—on the Eucharist, on Reconciliation, on sex, on birth control, on attitudes toward the Church, even on abortion and euthanasia, as well as on a host of other issues, but receive unsatisfactory answers, we must ask "Why?" Patrick J. Brennan offers suggestions as to how the RCIA *should* work (*Re-Imagining the Parish* 79–81), but does it? We need to assess rigorously the outcomes of our schooling and of RCIA instruction.

Evangelization, "Sharing the Good News"

Some might argue that emphasis on ecumenism has blunted the drive for converts or the effort to share the Good News of Christ with those outside the faith. We fail to attract blacks, to retain Hispanics, who drift to other churches, or to attract more than a fraction of the white non-Catholic population. *We appear unable to convince the general non-Catholic population to agree with our key moral positions.*

Some priests seem to feel that "evangelization" is "gauche" in a pluralistic society and not even a proper "Catholic" term. Father Patrick Brennan refutes these claims (*The Evangelizing Parish* 8–12). He is not alone. Archbishop Thomas Murphy calls for "committing resources and personnel to a ministry of evangelization" (656), and certainly in *Evangelii Nuntiandi* Pope Paul VI placed evangelization at the very center of the Church's reason for being.

The Vocation Crisis

We need to revive the tripartite pursuit of vocations: parents, pastors, and instructors (RCIA, schools) need to be enlisted—not in a Madison Avenue "hard sell" manner, but by creating a climate of spiritual growth, respect, appreciation, and encouragement for the priesthood and religious life. Dioceses need to restore the vocation modeling and the approachability of priests, unfortunately damaged by pedophilia scandals (Dudley and Laurent).

The Loss of Pastoral Symbols

Choices made for cogent reasons sometimes have unexpected consequences. The loss of some form of uniform habit (however modern and updated) for religious women was well intended and may have succeeded in its purpose (Quinonez and Turner 42, 55, 84, 89, 121, 159). Yet one of the most universally recognized religious symbols of our culture was lost, and religious sisters virtually disappeared from sight. That specific issue is moot; lost symbols are rarely regained.

The question is, What have we learned? What other symbols are fading? Should they? Is this dismissal by choice or by chance? How might this loss apply to religious devotions? To liturgical styles? To honoring the saints? To clerical garb?

Sanctity of Life

Pastors have been fighting for the sanctity of life especially hard since *Roe v. Wade.* Yet more than thirty-five million abortions have occurred (Charen; Schaffer) or about *five times the victims of the Holocaust!* Is that success? *What about end of life, the next great battlefield over the sanctity of life?*

Ethicist Peter Singer and medical doctors such as Dr. Sherwin B. Nuland believe and instruct others that we are little more than advanced animals—and expendable. But eight years of observing nursing home care virtually every day empirically reinforced my faith view that we have much to gain in honoring the sanctity of life and that God uses our lives well even to the very last breath, even when we are helpless (Mahoney, "Lessons from a Rose"). Impaired lives can still draw love from caregivers and others, helping to change them for the better.

Summary Comments

How may the Catholic Church best serve the souls in its care? I have reviewed a brief history of pastoral sociology, a development of the second half of the twentieth century, and have provided links to pastoral research resources; I have reviewed some sample results from a specific pastoral research study and reflected on questions raised. Finally, I have listed a few of the many areas of special pastoral concern and need facing us at the threshold of the new millennium.

Pastoral sociology has the tools to explore these issues in helpful ways. Pastors and parishes must seek and support research at all levels and must use the results wisely and with vigor both in policy and practice. The success or failure of this effort will have a pivotal effect on the Catholic Church in the United States throughout this new millennium. We must keep in mind the CARA inspiration taken from the "Pastoral Constitution on the Church in the Modern World": "In pastoral care, sufficient use should be made, not only of theological principles, but also of the findings of secular sciences, especially psychology and sociology: in this way the faithful will be brought to a purer and more mature living of the faith" (*Gaudium et Spes* 62).

WORKS CITED

Brennan, Patrick J. *The Evangelizing Parish*. Allen, Tex.: Tabor, 1987.

———. *Re-Imagining the Parish*. New York: Crossroad, 1990.

Castelli, Jim, and Gremillion, Joseph. *The Emerging Parish: The Notre Dame Study of Catholic Life Since Vatican II*. San Francisco: Harper and Row, 1987.

Catholic Research Forum. "Mission." Available at: http://www.execpc.com/~mcieslak/crf/mission.htm.

Center for Applied Research in the Apostolate. *The Cara Story*. Washington, D.C.: CARA, 1999.

Charen, Mona. "Pro-Abortion Movement Must Count Its Losses." *Insight on the News* 16, no. 5 (Feb. 7, 2000): 44–45.

CNN.com. "Bishops Discuss Growing Priest Shortage, Criminal Justice." June 16, 2000.

———. "Priest Shortage as Membership Surges." June 18, 2000.

Cochran, John K., and Leonard Beeghley. "The Influence of Religion on Attitudes toward Nonmarital Sexuality: A Preliminary Assessment of Reference Group Therapy." *Journal for the Scientific Study of Religion* 30, no. 1 (March 1991): 45–62.

Dolan, Jay P., R. S. Appleby, P. Byrne, and D. Campbell. *Transforming Parish Ministry*. New York: Crossroad, 1990.

Dudley, Roger L., and C. Robert Laurent. "Alienation from Religion in Church-Related Adolescents." *Sociological Analysis* 49, no. 4 (winter 1989): 408–20.

Fichter, Joseph H., S.J. *Dynamics of a City Church*. Chicago: University of Chicago Press, 1951.

———. *One-Man Research: Reminiscences of a Catholic Sociologist*. New York: John Wiley and Sons, 1973.

Froehle, Bryan T., and Mary L. Gautier, eds. *Catholicism USA: A Portrait of the Catholic Church in the United States*. Maryknoll, N.Y.: Orbis, 2000.

Gaudium et Spes. December 7, 1965.

Greeley, Andrew M. *The Catholic Myth: The Behavior and Beliefs of American Catholics*. 1990. Reprint. New York: Simon and Schuster, 1997.

———. *The Communal Catholic: A Personal Manifesto*. New York: Seabury, 1976.

———. *Religious Change in America*. 1989. Reprint. Cambridge, Mass.: Harvard University Press, 1996.

———. "Sociology and the Catholic Church: Four Decades of Bitter Memories." *Sociological Analysis* 50, no. 4 (1989): 393–97.

Hoge, Dean R., Joseph J. Shields, and Douglas L. Griffin. "Changes in Satisfaction and Institutional Attitudes of Catholic Priests, 1970–1993." *Sociology of Religion* 56, no. 2 (1995): 195–213.

Hoge, Dean R., J. Shields, and Mary Jeanne Verdieck. "Changing Age Distribution and Theological Attitudes of Catholic Priests." *Sociological Analysis* 49, no. 3 (fall 1988): 264–80.

Houtart, François. *Sociology and Pastoral Care*. Translated by Malachy Carroll. Chicago: Franciscan Herald, 1965.

Laumann, Edward O., John H. Gagnon, Robert T. Michael, and Stuart Michaels. *The Social Organization of Sexuality: Sexual Practices in the United States*. Chicago: University of Chicago Press, 1994.

McNamara, Patrick. "American Catholicism in the Mid-Eighties: Pluralism and Conflict in a Changing Church." *Annals of the American Academy of Political and Social Science* 480 (July 1985): 63–74.

Mahoney, Robert J. "Lessons from a Rose: Sociological Reflections on Eight Years of Long-Term Care." *Illness, Crisis, and Loss* 7, no. 1 (January 1999): 77–90.

———. "Pluralism or Polarity? Currents in a Catholic Parish." Paper presented at the meeting of the Religious Research Association, St. Louis, Missouri, 1995.

———. "Working Paper #8." *Parish Study Series*, 1993. Unpublished data.

Massa, Mark S. *Catholics and American Culture.* New York: Crossroad, 1999.

Murphy, Archbishop Thomas. "Signs of Hope: Focal Points for Pastoral Planners." *Origins* 21, no. 41 (March 19, 1992): 653, 655–58.

Nuland, Sherwin B. *How We Die: Reflections on Life's Final Chapter.* New York: Alfred A. Knopf, 1993.

The Official Catholic Directory: Anno Domini 1998. New Providence, N.J.: P. J. Kennedy and Sons, 1998.

Pardun, Carol J., and Kathy B. McKee. "Strange Bedfellows: Symbols of Religion and Sexuality on MTV." *Youth and Society* 26, no. 4 (June 1995): 438–49.

Paul VI. *Evangelii Nuntiandi.* December 8, 1975.

Petersen, Larry R., and Gregory V. Donnenwerth. "Secularization and the Influence of Religion on Beliefs about Premarital Sex." *Social Forces* 75, no. 3 (March 1997): 1071–88.

Potvin, Raymond H. *Seminarians of the 80s: A National Survey.* Washington, D.C.: National Catholic Educational Association, 1986.

Quinonez, Lora Ann, C.D.P., and Mary Daniel Turner, S.N.D.-deN. *The Transformation of American Catholic Sisters.* Philadelphia: Temple University Press, 1992.

Raymond, Brother John. *Catholics on the Internet: 2000–2001.* Roseville, Calif.: Prima, 2000.

Rigney, Daniel, and Thomas J. Hoffman. "Is American Catholicism Anti-Intellectual?" *Journal for the Scientific Study of Religion* 32, no. 3 (September 1993): 211–22.

Schaffer, Bob. "27 Years of *Roe v. Wade:* Justice to All Living Humans, Born and Unborn." *Vital Speeches of the Day* 66, no. 9 (February 15, 2000): 281–84.

Schoenherr, Richard A., and Annemette Sorensen. "Social

Change in Religious Organizations: Consequences of Clergy Decline in the U.S. Catholic Church." *Sociological Analysis* 43, no. 1 (spring 1982): 23–52.

Schoenherr, Richard A., and Lawrence A. Young. *Full Pews and Empty Altars: Demographics of the Priest Shortage in United States Catholic Dioceses*. Madison: University of Wisconsin Press, 1993.

Singer, Peter. *Rethinking Life and Death: The Collapse of Our Traditional Ethics*. New York: St. Martin's, 1994.

Sly, Julie. "Eucharist 'Answers Hurts, Doubts, Despair.'" *The Catholic Key* 32, no. 15 (April 16, 2000): 1.

Sweetser, Thomas P., and Carol W. Holden. *Leadership in a Successful Parish*. San Francisco: HarperSanFrancisco, 1986.

Sweetser, Thomas P., and Mary Benet McKinney. *Changing Pastors: A Resource for Pastoral Transitions*. Kansas City, Mo.: Sheed and Ward, 1998.

Verdieck, Mary Jeanne, Joseph J. Shields, and Dean R. Hoge. "Role Commitment Processes Revisited; American Catholic Priests 1970 and 1985." *Journal for the Scientific Study of Religion* 27, no. 4 (December 1988): 524–35.

Wakin, Edward, and Joseph F. Scheuer. *The De-Romanization of the American Catholic Church*. Westport, Conn.: Greenwood, 1966.

Wallace, Ruth A. *They Call Her Pastor: A New Role for Catholic Women*. Albany: State University of New York, 1992.

Wicks, Robert J., and Thomas E. Rodgerson. *Companions in Hope: The Art of Christian Caring*. New York: Paulist, 1998.

Young, Lawrence A., Richard A. Schoenherr, Dean R. Hoge, Joseph J. Shields, and Mary Jeanne Verdieck. "The Changing Age Distribution and Theological Attitudes of Catholic Priests Revisited." *Sociological Analysis* 53, no. 1 (spring 1992): 73–87.

Yuhaus, Cassian, ed. *The Catholic Church and American Culture: Reciprocity and Challenge*. Mahwah, N.J.: Paulist, 1990.

FOUR
Social Justice

7

Catholic Social Teaching at the Millennium: The Human Condition in Light of the Gospel

Gerald L. Miller

To Our Venerable Brethren the Patriarchs, Primates, Archbishops, Bishops, and other ordinaries of places having Peace and Communion with the Apostolic See.

That the spirit of revolutionary change, which has long been disturbing the nations of the world, should have passed beyond the sphere of politics and made its influence felt in the cognate sphere of practical economics is not surprising. The elements of the conflict now raging are unmistakable, in the vast expansion of industrial pursuits and the marvelous discoveries of science; in the changed relations between masters and workmen; in the enormous fortunes of some few individuals, and the utter poverty of the masses; the increased self reliance and closer mutual combination of the working classes; as also, finally, in the prevailing moral degeneracy. The momentous gravity of the state of things now obtaining fills every mind with painful apprehension; wise men are discussing it; practical men are proposing schemes; popular meetings, legislatures, and rulers of nations are all busied with it— actually there is no question which has taken deeper hold on the public mind.

. . .

In regard to the Church, her cooperation will never be found lacking, be the time or the occasion what it may; . . . she will intervene. . . . Let this be carefully

taken to heart by those whose office it is to safeguard
the public welfare. Every minister of holy religion
must bring to the struggle the full energy of his mind
and all of his power of endurance.

—Pope Leo XIII, *Rerum Novarum*

SADLY, many Catholics are unaware of what a rich history regarding social commentary and teaching we have in the Roman
Catholic Church today, at the millennium. In the modern era,
Catholic social teaching dates back to Pope Leo XIII, whose cou-
rageous 1891 papal encyclical *Rerum Novarum* (New Things),
subtitled *On the Condition of the Working Classes,* started the current tradition of popes, cardinals, bishops, priests, religious and
laypersons, and the Church in general commenting on the economic and social aspects of the societies and cultures around the
globe, in which the Church exists. What Leo XIII was attempting
to do through *Rerum Novarum* was to consider the effects of
these *new things* that were coming along with the Industrial Revolution, capitalism, and socialism, especially in terms of how
these developments affected the working class. *Things,* such as a
just wage, were dealt with, in addition to the right of workers to
organize, the rights of property, and the rights of property owners. All of these issues were *things* that the Church weighed the
effects of in any society.

Fast forward to the year 2000: now Catholics have a tradition
of more than one hundred years of social and economic commentary, with scores of encyclicals, papal documents, and bishops' pastoral letters, all known collectively as "Catholic social
teaching." And just what is "Catholic social teaching"? Truly,
its essence can be captured in a very few words: *commentary on
the human condition in light of the Gospel* (see Schultheis).

The human condition in light of the Gospel—that is an excellent short statement of what Catholic social teaching is really all
about. What is our condition—as human beings in today's society, in light of or from the perspective of the Gospel, from the
perspective of Christ, from the perspective of loving one another
as God has loved us—the human condition in light of the
Gospel?

Human Dignity

> At the summit of creation stands the creation of man and woman, made in God's image (Gen. 1:26–27). As such every human being possesses an inalienable dignity that stamps human existence prior to any division into races or nations and prior to human labor and human achievement (Gen. 4:11).
>
> —*Economic Justice for All*

Catholic social teaching has, as its main girder, a concept referred to throughout all of recorded human history—*dignitas*, or dignity, the quintessential value that all human beings have by virtue of their creation, by virtue of their being called into existence by God with their names written in the Creator's hand. All human beings have dignity by virtue of their birth, created in the image and likeness of God. Dignity that is inalienable and inviolate. Dignity that cannot be taken away and cannot be given away.

Being created in God's image and likeness does not necessarily mean that we physically look like God. It could be that we are created in God's image and likeness in terms of our psychological, emotional, and spiritual selves, in terms of the emotions that we can feel and experience, the spirituality of our lives. We do know from God, from both the Old Testament and the New Testament, that we have been created, all of us, each of us, as individuals in the image and likeness of God. And by that fact alone, by virtue of our creation in the image and likeness of God, no other appeal to any other reasons is required: *we all have human dignity*.

This dignity affords all people certain necessary minimums, along with certain rights and responsibilities, to allow us to achieve, to live out, this human dignity in our actual environment, in the larger society. Consider, by way of example, the first ten amendments to the Constitution, known as the Bill of Rights, every American's minimum constitutional and political rights. In the United States, all citizens have, by virtue of being U.S. citizens, these basic rights.

In like manner, all people have rights to certain economic and social minimums based on human dignity. Catholic social teaching has attempted to establish these certain economic and social rights that we all have, the required minimums that all persons need to achieve human dignity. Catholic social teaching has attempted to establish an economic and social Bill of Rights for all peoples in all places.

Option for the Poor and Vulnerable

> *All members of society have a special obligation to the poor and vulnerable. . . .* This "option for the poor" does not mean pitting one group against another, but rather strengthening the whole community by assisting those who are most vulnerable. As Christians we are called to respond to the needs of *all* our brothers and sisters, but those with the greatest need require the greatest response.
>
> —*Economic Justice for All*

The first important theme of Catholic social teaching to discuss is a preferential option for the poor, a very difficult concept for many people to understand for a variety of reasons. The terminology is sufficiently foreign enough from common usage that the naming of the concept leaves many people with little or no real understanding of the deep message *it conveys*.

Essentially what "a preferential option for the poor" means is that when we vote, when we participate in making policy for businesses or civic associations, when we make a decision, whether it be through a home association, a political process, or a board of directors, we must consider the impact that vote, that policy, that decision has on those who are least capable of protecting themselves—the poor, the marginalized, the powerless.

Consider the incredible opportunity for a preferential option for the poor the U.S. economy presently offers. During fiscal year 2000, as a nation, we enjoyed our second national budget surplus in a row. For a second year, the U.S. government actually took in more tax money at the federal level than it spent. This development turns around literally years and years, decades, of federal budget deficits, wherein the United States spent a great deal more than was taken in through taxes. In fact, the federal budget deficit grew so large in 1991 that there was almost $300 billion more spending than in taxes collected. Many Americans were really afraid that this deficit was going to continue to balloon to half a trillion dollars and go up from there, not only leading to large budget deficits but also necessitating huge increases in federal debt.

Now, in our current fabulously robust economy, there are federal budget surpluses. In February 2000, the U.S. economy had achieved 107 consecutive months of economic growth, which is the longest economic expansion in the recorded history of the United States, whether in a time of war or not. This is a tremendous economy, a fabulously strong, robust economy, which has done a great deal to lower poverty and unemployment rates through generating better-paying jobs for many people.

This record economic expansion has now even brought the United States to the point where we are dealing with budget surpluses, actually taking more in through taxes at the federal level because people who were on welfare are now gainfully employed taxpayers. Indeed, these surpluses are now projected to continue to the point that the United States might have no federal debt, no publicly held debt whatsoever by the year 2013. And, if in fact we do pay off the debt by 2013 with these budget surpluses, it would be the first time since Andrew "Old Hickory" Jackson was president in 1835 that the national government had no debt.

But should debt payment be all that the government does with these budget surpluses? Or should, as politicians try to impress voters for political popularity, the government return these budget surpluses in the form of tax cuts? Assume that the politicians decide to lower taxes, the very politically popular thing to do. Obviously, if the federal government is experiencing budget surpluses, we can afford tax cuts. Then, based on a preferential option for the poor, should we try to take into account *how* the United States is going to return this money back to the economy, back to the people?

Tax monies could be given back in such a way that there would not necessarily be, say, a 10 percent tax cut across the board. Possibly there might be a 5 percent tax cut for the upper-income households and a 25 percent, 30 percent, or 40 percent tax cut for the lower-income households. That's how a preferential option for the poor could work in this case. A preferential option for the poor involves making a decision that has a differential impact on the poor, a decision that shows a preference to the poor, a decision that allows the poor to have hope of eventually escaping their poverty and their powerlessness.

The Diocese of Kansas City–St. Joseph, Missouri, has been making a preferential option for the poor with its Central City School Fund, where monies are collected in order to keep inner-city Catholic schools open, schools that would otherwise close without such extra financing. This is an example of the Church not turning its back on the poor, but exercising a preferential option for the poor. Not all of the Catholic schools in the diocese receive this preferential treatment or extra infusion of funding, but the inner-city schools do to help them stay open and to provide the central city with quality Catholic education. That is what a preferential option for the poor is when we vote. When we make decisions, when we make policies, we build in from the very beginning a preferential impact on the poor and the powerless through our votes, our decisions, and our policies.

RIGHTS AND RESPONSIBILITIES

> In a world where some speak mostly of "rights" and others mostly of "responsibilities," the Catholic tradition teaches that human dignity can be protected and a healthy community can be achieved only if human rights are protected and responsibilities are met. Therefore, every person has a fundamental right to life and a right to those things required for human decency. Corresponding to these rights are duties and responsibilities—to one another, to our families, and to the larger society.
>
> —*Sharing Catholic Social Teaching*

Another theme of Catholic social teaching centers on rights and responsibilities. Although the discussion deals with rights first, it is important to understand from the very beginning that responsibilities are equally important. These rights are not without accompanying responsibilities.

What are these rights? They are the rights, economically and socially, that are needed and necessary as minimums to provide for human dignity. The first right is the right to be born. One can visualize the right to be born defended in an arm-in-arm march by right-to-life organizations, the pro-lifers—an important living out of our beliefs. There are, however, other rights, too. Sometimes, after a child is born, one-issue Christians drift off to the sidelines; they break the arm-in-arm approach of defending human rights and go back home. But after the right to be born, other rights need to be championed also: the right to good nutrition, the right to a functional education, the right to a decent job paying a living wage, the right to adequate health care, and the right to a safe home. We need to work toward the achievement of certain minimums that are part of an economic and social Bill of Rights and are necessary for true human dignity.

The right to be born. Yes, the right to be born is fundamental, but so too is the right once born to sufficient nutrition, the right to a program such as Head Start, which helps poor and disadvantaged children to move forward with a hot meal and extra learning assistance in preschool and to move successfully into the traditional school system.

The right to adequate health care. It is estimated that forty-four million Americans are without health care insurance at this very moment—forty-four million—and many of those are children, millions and millions of children. This is not right. A country as rich as the United States ought to be able to provide health care for everyone, especially all children.

The right to a good education. Sadly, many students who actually graduate—who actually attend faithfully, do their work and graduate with a diploma—receive an education that leaves them functionally illiterate. They graduate with a diploma that does not translate into any marketable skills the economy wants. Students who work at learning in order to be successful have a right to a good education, an education that yields functional skills capable of being marketed gainfully to the economy. The responsibility the students have is to work at it, to study, to try, and the parents have to be part of the process, too. As ironic as it sounds, for many teachers in elementary and secondary schools, the obstacles to a good education for their students are the parents themselves. Parents need to support the educational process; parents need to work with their children to make sure that their homework gets done and that they are going to school consistently, rested, fed, and attentive.

The right to productive employment. What is meant by "productive employment"? It is meaningful employment that will pay, as an example, for a father, a mother, and two minor children a decent wage, a living wage, a *just wage*, sometimes termed a *family wage.* Those who are willing to trade their entire full-time work life for forty to forty-five years or more have the right, based on human dignity, to lift themselves and their families out of poverty.

The right to secure a living wage is just not feasible at today's minimum wage of $5.15 an hour or $10,712 dollars yearly. Furthermore, there is no possibility that the family of four is going to be anything but impoverished by our own national standards given the current federal government's poverty threshold for a family of four of approximately $17,000 a year (U.S. Census Bureau). Earning slightly more than $17,000 annually will not extract this small family from real poverty, even if they are formally over the poverty thresholds. $17,500 a year for a family of four is still poverty indeed.

All people have a right, if they are willing to trade their work life for forty to forty-five years or more, to earn a living wage that will afford the family some measure of dignity. These very same people have a responsibility to work, to be part of the economy, to be dependable if they are able bodied. In return, they have the right to a living wage, a family wage, a wage that will allow a small family to be raised in dignity and not in poverty.

The right to a dignified retirement. Persons who have worked their entire lives—who have given their entire work lives faithfully to the economy—also have the right to a respectable retirement: a retirement that has satisfactory health care insurance; a retirement that affords comfortable, safe housing; a retirement that has heat in the winter and air-conditioning in the summer; a retirement that has ample food. These are the sorts of things we all want for ourselves during our retirement years.

Interspersed in the enumeration of these rights have been some of the responsibilities: to be part of the educational process, to work full-time if able bodied, to be dependable. If we are willing to contribute fully to society in the manner that the fulfillment of human dignity demands, then we also have the right to achieve certain economic and social minimums—certain necessary rights are to be satisfied regarding shelter, health care, education, and employment that pays a living, family wage.

SOLIDARITY

"I give you a new commandment: love one another. As I have loved you, so you also should love one another. This is how all will know that you are my disciples, if you have love for one another" (Jn. 13:34–35). . . . What the Bible and Christian tradition teach, human wisdom confirms. Centuries before Christ, the Greeks and Romans spoke of the human person as a "social animal" made for friendship, community and public life. These insights show that human beings achieve self-realization not in isolation, but in interaction with others. . . . Solidarity is another name for this social friendship and civic commitment that make human moral and economic life possible.

—Economic Justice for All

Solidarity is another important theme of Catholic social teaching. Solidarity is, in many ways, the theme most difficult to really internalize, to actually feel what the Church is trying to convey by it. One way to think about solidarity is in terms of the kinds of projects initiated for children to do in elementary and secondary schools: collecting for the poor and homeless, collecting warm blankets and clothing, collecting canned food and money for the poor are all valuable ways of helping the poor.

But whether it be collecting warm clothes or canned food, many times the vital next step is not taken, the necessary tie-in that helps the elementary and high school students to recognize why there needs to be such collections of warm blankets, clothes, or canned food. In other words, solidarity requires more than bringing canned food in order to get a dress-down day or a homework pass or a pizza party for the class that collected the most food. These efforts on behalf of the poor need to be connected to an appreciation of Catholic social teaching—that we are, as Christ's followers, trying to stand in solidarity with the poor by sharing with them what we are able to.

Solidarity goes even deeper than this. Reflect on the idea of the *precarity* of poverty. Dorothy Day, one of the cofounders of the Catholic Worker Movement in the United States, often talked about how she was trying to move from a *spirit* of poverty to knowing the *"precarity"* of poverty (Day 106–9). Precariousness could refer to how a boulder is teetering dangerously, ready to fall down a mountainside. Precariousness conveys the feeling that the boulder might tip and roll down the mountain *at any time*. Dorothy Day wanted people not only to care for the poor, but to realize that their lives teetered precariously and, *at any time*, could roll down the mountain into disaster.

The *precarity* of poverty: that in a spirit of poverty we would not only understand what it is like to be laughed at for wearing mismatched clothes from a thrift shop or driving an oil-guzzling, smoke-spewing dented wreck of a car to the first job *and* to the second job, but at an even deeper level would comprehend that even this life of thrift shop clothes and smoke-belching, beat up cars is absolutely precarious. A sudden illness, an unforeseen lay-off at work, and it would all roll down hill into disaster. Almost any problem at all, a problem that most of the nonpoor would ride out easily, could send this precarious life teetering and falling down the mountainside *immediately*. The precarious house of cards would collapse.

Dorothy Day wanted us to *feel*, by use of the notion of the *precarity* of poverty, that grinding poverty is like ubiquitous elevator music in the background; the precariousness, even when things are seemingly going well, is always there. She wanted us to internalize what the poor always know: they could be homeless within a day or two, that even this little shabby life they have put together could all fall apart in no time. As Day wrote in 1952, "Nowadays religious communities are good, I am sure, but they are mistaken about poverty. They accept, admit, poverty on principle, but everything must be good and strong, buildings must be fireproof. Precarity is everywhere rejected, and *precarity is an essential element of poverty*" (Day 108, italics mine).

A further approach to deepening our understanding of being in solidarity with the poor would be to consider and reflect on what the poor—if they had the opportunity to speak or write through us, use our voice, use our keyboard—would say or write to the rest of us. How can we say what being in solidarity with the poor means? What would the poor want all peoples to hear? What would they want us to realize? When we can honestly grasp this notion, a true understanding of solidarity with the poor begins.

Finally, the deepest realization of solidarity comes through a genuine appreciation of the Mystical Body of Christ. As with our own bodies, we, all of us, are literally parts of this larger whole. Whether it be a little toe or a finger, a lung, or an ear, they are all important parts of the body, and if a toe or a lung is hurt, the whole body suffers. If we are sincerely in solidarity with the poor, the marginalized, the powerless, to the point of recognizing all peoples as part of Christ's Mystical Body, then when the poor suffer, the whole body suffers; we all truly suffer, even out in the suburbs, even in our heated and air-conditioned homes, even with our plentiful food.

How can we understand what it is like to be poor? How can we internalize the suffering of the poor and powerless, the precarity of their poverty? How can we say what the poor would want us to say, what they would say if only they were listened to? How can we hurt until they are healed? We can do so only through real solidarity with the poor as part of the Mystical Body of Christ.

STEWARDSHIP

The fact [is] that God has given the earth for the use and enjoyment of the whole human race. . . . Moreover, the earth, even though apportioned among pri-

vate owners, ceases not thereby to minister to the
needs of all, inasmuch as there is not one who does
not sustain life from what the land produces.

. . .

[There is a] chief and most excellent rule for the
right use of money . . . which the Church has traced
out clearly, and has not only made known to men's
minds, but has impressed upon their lives. It rests on
the principle that it is one thing to have the right to the
possession of money and another to have a right to use
money as one wills. Private ownership . . . is the natural right of man, and to exercise that right, especially
as members of society, is not only lawful, but absolutely necessary. "It is lawful," says St. Thomas Aquinas, "for a man to hold private property; and it is also
necessary for the carrying on of human existence." But
if the question be asked: How must one's possessions
be used?—the Church replies without hesitation in the
words of the same holy Doctor: "Man should not consider his material possessions as his own, but as common to all, so as to share them without hesitation
when others are in need. . . . True, no one is com-
manded to distribute to others that which is required
for his own needs and those of his household; nor
even to give away what is reasonably required to keep
up becomingly his condition in life, "for no one ought
to live other than becomingly." But, when what necessity demands has been supplied, and one's standing
fairly taken [care of] . . . , it becomes a duty to give to
the indigent out of what remains over. . . . To sum up,
what has been said: Whoever has received from the
divine bounty a large share of temporal blessings,
whether they be external and material, or gifts of the
mind, has received them for the purpose of using them
for the perfecting of his own nature, and, at the same
time, that he may employ them, as the steward of
God's providence, for the benefit of others. "He that
hath talent," said St. Gregory the Great, "let him see
that he hide it not; he that hath abundance, let him
quicken himself to mercy and generosity; he that hath
art and skill, let him do his best to share the use and
the utility hereof with his neighbor."

—Pope Leo XIII, *Rerum Novarum*

Stewardship is sometimes a code word in the Catholic Church for giving money—that people be good stewards of what they have been given, that they respond to a stewardship appeal and pledge monies to whatever it is that is being campaigned for—but it is so much deeper than this.

First, there is stewardship of the environment. We all have a responsibility to leave the gifts of God on this earth in as good or better condition than we found them. After all, really the earth is not ours. We are stewards. The earth is a gift; it is all a gift from God.

A house sits on a piece of land. Now, by the legal definition of things, someone owns that piece of land. But does that person really own it? In other words, does she have the right to do anything with that piece of land she so chooses? Legally, maybe. Because she has title to the land, she could potentially take uranium tailings and spread them all over the lot, which would poison the land and leave it radioactive for literally eons to come. Nobody could use it. Maybe legally she could do that. She has the title to that piece of property. But it is really not her piece of property. She did not create it.

No one really *owns* pieces of the earth, even if he or she has legal title to them. The earth was a creation, a gift of God, and we do not have the right to take gifts of God and destroy them or hoard them and do just anything we want with them. We need to be good stewards, good stewards of this earth so that we do not pollute it and so that we do not use up all of its nonrenewable resources in our lifetimes. There simply cannot be this continued greedy sprawl, more and more for us and less and less for wilderness, for the future. It is all a gift. It is all given. We do not own the earth or the minerals or the climate or the forests.

Stewardship is even more than this; it's about all of our human gifts, too. Someone's ability to speak, to stand up in front of people and talk, or another's athletic abilities, business abilities, teaching abilities, parenting abilities—they are all gifts. We did not wish our ability package on ourselves or create it for ourselves, even if we have worked hard to develop it. We are given different gifts, but we are all given gifts, gifts from God, and good stewardship tells us that, as with the land, we cannot hoard them, they cannot just be for us. We cannot take our gifts and just use them in a way that only makes us money for our selfish self interests. They are gifts—we did not create them, we did not give them to ourselves, we do not own them, and good stewardship requires that we share them with the rest of humankind, for the common good of everyone. Stewardship complements the theme of solidarity within the Mystical Body of Christ—that we are all part of this larger whole and that we are to use all of these gifts in good stewardship for everyone in that Mystical Body.

SOCIAL JUSTICE

> Justice also has implications for the way the larger social, economic and political institutions of society are organized. *Social justice implies that persons have an obligation to be active and productive participants in the life of society and that society has a duty to enable them to participate in this way.*
>
> —*Economic Justice for All* (italics in original)

And if we ever achieve this dignity, it is only justice, not charity. It is not charity to respond positively to Catholic social teaching; it is not out of the charity of our hearts that we choose to provide these minimums, that we choose solidarity, that we choose to be good stewards to help the poor with our gifts, that we choose a preference for the poor in our decisions. To respond to this call so that all can live with some human dignity is to respond to the call of justice.

As a nation, we have responded to the call that all Americans should have the right to vote; we would fight for the belief that all Americans have a right to certain freedoms based on the Bill of Rights. In like manner, to work for all people to achieve these economic and social minimums is not charity; it is not simply the goodness of our hearts. It is justice, it is the way that it should be, it is working for the kind of society that should exist. *Social justice* is providing for human dignity within the society itself. A society that would rob any member of human dignity is not a just society, and therefore there is a social injustice. So when we work for social justice, we are working to provide each other human dignity, and it is only just that all are able live with some dignity.

CONCLUSION

The main themes of Catholic social teaching sum up to this: by virtue of our creation by God, who called us from nothingness to birth, to life, to creation, in God's own image and likeness, we—all of us, each and every one of us—have dignity. Human dignity—inalienable and inviolable—cannot be given away and cannot be taken away. Because we have dignity by virtue of our creation, there are certain things, necessary minimum aspects of economic and social life, that are required to support the true achievement of this dignity. Collectively captured, the main themes of Catholic social teaching are:

A preferential option for the poor—to help those who are poor, marginalized, and powerless one day to become full members of society.

Rights and responsibilities—those necessary minimums for dignity also include the responsibility to be part of the process of providing these rights.

Solidarity—to understand literally that all of us are part of a larger whole, parts of the Mystical Body of Christ, and that whatever hurts any of us harms us all.

And, finally, *stewardship*—the knowledge that all is gift, and, as good stewards, we cannot hoard our gifts; we cannot be ever greedy for more for us only.

In the new millennium, Catholic social teaching must continue to respond to the needs of all humans in light of the Gospel. As the Church teaches, we must be good stewards; we must share in a preferential way and in solidarity with all people in order to help secure those necessary rights, with their accompanying responsibilities, that all humans need for true human dignity.

WORKS CITED

Day, Dorothy. *Dorothy Day: Selected Writings*. Edited by Robert Ellsberg. Maryknoll, N.Y.: Orbis, 1997.

Economic Justice for All: Catholic Social Teaching and the U.S. Economy. U.S. bishops' pastoral message and letter, November 27. Washington, D.C.: National Catholic News Service, 1986.

Pope Leo XIII. *Rerum Novarum*. May 15, 1891.

Schultheis, Michael J., Edward P. DeBerri, and Peter J. Henriot. *Our Best Kept Secret: The Rich Heritage of Catholic Social Teaching*. Washington, D.C.: Center of Concern, 1987.

Sharing Catholic Social Teaching: Challenges and Directions. Reflections of the U.S. Catholic bishops, June. Washington, D.C.: United States Catholic Conference, 1998.

U.S. Census Bureau. *Current Population Survey*. P60 Series. February 1, 2000. Available: www.census.gov/hhes/poverty/threshld/thresh99.html.

8

Food Security and Catholic Social Teaching

Laura E. Fitzpatrick

EVERY 3.6 SECONDS someone somewhere in the world dies from hunger. Seventy-five percent of those who die are children under the age of five (HungerSite). As astounding, sobering, and frustrating as these figures are, they nevertheless underrepresent the magnitude of the hunger problem in this world. They do not include the multitudes who languish and suffer from hunger-related problems but who have not yet succumbed. That even one individual dies from hunger is tragic. That millions suffer and perhaps even die is both incomprehensible and a circumstance that demands a response. One call for such a response is found in Catholic social teaching.

CATHOLIC SOCIAL TEACHING

The foundation in Catholic social teaching for acting against the terrible toll hunger takes can be traced through three encyclicals. A recurring theme in each of the encyclicals *Rerum Novarum, Populorum Progressio,* and *Centesimus Annus* is that the fruits of the earth are for all to share. Further, this principle supercedes the "rights" created by humankind that would interfere with such sharing. In *Rerum Novarum,* one finds "the earth even though apportioned among private owners, ceases not thereby to minister to the needs of all, inasmuch as there is no one who does not sustain life from what the land produces" (Leo XIII 7). This sentiment is echoed in *Populorum Progressio.*

> Now if the earth has been created for the purpose of furnishing individuals either with the necessities of a livelihood or the means

of progress, it follows that each individual has the right to get from it what is necessary for that individual. . . . All other rights, whatever they are, including property rights and the right of free trade, must be subordinated to this norm; they must not hinder it, but must rather expedite its application. (Paul VI 22)

Finally, in *Centesimus Annus*, one finds that "the original source of all that is good is the very act of God, who created both the earth and human beings so that humans might have dominion over it by their work and enjoy its fruits (Genesis 1:28). God gave the earth to the whole human race for the sustenance of all its members without excluding anyone" (John Paul II 31).

We live in a world of plenty for parts of the population but of great suffering and privation for others. This lack of balance reflects a skewed access to the fruits of the earth. To the extent some are excluded from these fruits, Catholic social teaching calls us to override the impediments humans have created to allow everyone access to the earth. We are in good company in this struggle, for many have similarly seen the injustice in the distribution of the world's wealth and have acted to alleviate hunger. The World Food Council remains hopeful because it finds that "in the light of the experience of a number of developing countries . . . humanity can feed itself if it adopts the proper means. . . . These means depend on the political will of governments and the international community to win the common battle against hunger" (World Food Council 1).

The Causes and Solutions to Food Insecurity

The battle against hunger must begin with the identification of that which is to be vanquished. The first step is to determine what hunger is. Hunger is a manifestation of food insecurity or, conversely, a lack of food security. Although definitions of food security abound, a commonly adopted—though not the only— definition is that of the World Bank: "Food security has to do with access by all people at all times to enough food for an active and healthy life" (World Bank v). Once the problem has been defined, efforts to deal with hunger require the identification of its causes and then the design and implementation of appropriate solutions.

Many different causes have been advanced for food insecurity. These causes emerge from particular definitions of food security. For some, food insecurity arises from shortfalls in agricultural production or actual shortages of food. These supply difficulties may be attributable to drought, war, or inappropriate agricultural practices. Other researchers note sufficient production of food accompanying food insecurity and identify access-related causes of food insecurity, such as lack of purchasing power, lack of foreign exchange, or poverty in general. Although some focus simply on supply of food being a problem and others focus particularly on demand, there is a tendency to look at food insecurity as a combination of the two. For example, both inadequate production and foreign exchange constraints may be identified as causes of food insecurity.

Great effort has been dedicated to the alleviation of these various causes for hunger. Each proposed solution reflects a particular definition of food security and the identification of particular causes of food insecurity. Proposed solutions include international financing schemes, buffer stocking, food aid/relief, increased trade, self-sufficiency, redistribution of wealth, and increased growth or development.

- *International financing schemes* are directed at enabling nations that experience fluctuations in domestic consumption because of fluctuating prices to finance imports without creating a great strain on their foreign exchange reserves.
- *Buffer stocks* are stockpiles of food held to offset fluctuations in supply and thereby moderate fluctuations in price. Food aid can serve both as a food source in an emergency and as a promotion for development through the freeing up of resources for development objectives.
- *Promotion of trade* is seen as a stabilizer of food markets, which allows poor harvests in one area to be offset by high production in another.
- *Self-sufficiency* is proposed by those who see transportation difficulties, urban biases, international political

whims, and political relations within some countries as impediments to food security that can be addressed only by increased regional or national self-reliance.

- *Redistribution of wealth*, some propose, will allow more people to have access to available food.
- *Growth or development* is a process meant to expand the production and availability of food and other goods, enabling increased consumption in all areas.

Examination of these varied solutions reveals two things. First, although these solutions have different foci, they can be used together (and they *are* combined in various ways) in a cohesive way, much like pieces to a larger puzzle. They are for the most part noncontradictory. Second, most of the solutions proposed to address hunger deal with short-term manifestations of food insecurity, but there remains continued faith in the ability of economic growth—or, in other words, development—to provide food security in the long run. This confidence in growth to deal with hunger comes from the fundamental theories of development wherein underdevelopment is characterized by, among other things, hunger and development is the process whereby such characteristics of underdevelopment are shed. Economic growth produces expanded consumption possibilities—including those of food—across the economy. Food security is presumed to be produced and maintained through growth or development.

This is not to say that short-term food insecurity problems cannot arise during the process of development, but these problems are typically seen as aberrations attributable to factors external to economic development. If troubles related to food security emerge, they could be addressed through tools that would further contribute to modernization. These tools include increased trade, increased production—augmented through green revolution technologies—stocks of food, aid, and international financing schemes. One may have to deal with such impediments in the short-run, but development ultimately implies the provision of food security.

FOOD INSECURITY WORLDWIDE

Great effort and vast resources have been directed at the problem of food insecurity along the lines described above. In spite of these efforts and resources, the problem continues. Even in some cases considered "success stories" in those countries that have experienced some economic development, food insecurity persists.

In Sri Lanka, "real household consumption fell for most people on the island during the mid-period of the economic boom" (Herring 172). Similar patterns are reported for Botswana. Despite average growth rates of 11.8 percent since independence in Botswana, the "food security problem has been evident . . . throughout the post-independence period to the present time" (Cathie and Hermann 15).

These findings are echoed in Brazil, where "despite twenty years of significant economic growth . . . a majority of Brazilians find themselves less able now than in the mid-1960's to obtain their basic food requirements" (Hollist 231). In the Philippines, "during the past two or three decades . . . hunger and poverty appear to have increased" (Bread for the World 12–13), although gross national product (GNP) grew at annual rates as high as 5.5 percent (*World Resources* 237), attributable to the promotion of industrialization and agricultural growth (David 85).

Pakistan has also registered sustained economic growth in the face of hunger.

> Though Pakistan produces enough food to adequately feed its people hunger persists. . . . Since the early 1960's, Pakistan has experienced an annual economic growth of about 6 percent and a significant increase in national food production. Yet more than half the children under five are underweight. . . . It is clear that poor nutrition and poverty are widespread in Pakistan in both urban and rural areas. (Bread for the World 33)

In Indonesia, growth rates of 6 to 7 percent (Booth and Baharsyah 1; *World Resources* 237) were recorded, but "undernutrition remains a serious problem . . . particularly among children. Half of all children under five are underweight." Furthermore, "the percentage of underweight children younger than 5 has not changed" (Bread for the World 22).

Observation of these countries reveals that although progress in modernization has occurred by traditional standards such as increased GNP, increased industrialization, increased trade, and increased participation in the world market, such progress has been accompanied by decreasing subsistence food production not offset by alternative sources, increasing levels of hunger and malnutrition, and rising levels of food insecurity. Food problems continue to exist and persist in spite of what has been considered progress away from the primary cause of food insecurity: economic underdevelopment.

Redefining the Concept of Food Security

The difficulty in eliminating food insecurity may not lie in the magnitude of resources utilized or in a lack of effort from those seeking to end it, but rather in how those people identify or envision the problem and how they seek to alleviate it. Perhaps the problem is not being solved because the problem is not perceived or analyzed in a manner that would permit formulation of solutions leading to its eradication.

Defining food insecurity as a characteristic of underdevelopment and delineating a universal path for proceeding from this state eliminates the need to consider the possibilities of alternative conceptions of food security. There is no room for divergence of interpretations within different contexts of what constitutes food, what constitutes enough food, and what constitutes a healthy and productive life—all terms used originally to define food security. There is no room to interpret differently what security means as settings change. There is no room to account for the diversity among societies and for all the different and distinct factors that affect these many societies.

Many examples lead one to question whether expanding the concept of food and security does not also require a reassessment of solutions to food insecurity. What food is and what constitutes enough food varies widely among cultures. Yellow corn—a staple of the U.S. diet—is considered fodder in some parts of the world and sending it as sustenance is not seen as a solution to food insecurity. For twenty years, the so-called perfect food in the United States—milk—served as a foundation for nutritional assistance around the world. The only problem is that Asians revile it culturally and up to 75 percent of the world's black population cannot physiologically tolerate it (Harris 130–32). In Poland, meat consumption is critical. Meeting World Health Organization standards for protein consumption and matching average calorie consumption levels in the United States is insufficient for maintaining the social order in that country. Even when such consumption levels were met, the Polish diet remained short of meat, resulting in social unrest (Harris 19–20).

Understanding cultural differences with respect to food and sufficiency of it is only the first step in solving the problem of food insecurity. We must look at the particular cultural, political, environmental, and economic factors that vary between societies to understand wherein lies a particular food insecurity and to devise an appropriate solution. This tactic differs from the traditional approach in that these factors are not impediments to the "real" solution, but rather the key to devising the culturally appropriate solution.

One example that illustrates a number of these factors is that of Somalia in the early 1990s. A traditional approach saw food insecurity in Somalia as resulting from low caloric consumption; hence, great quantities of food were shipped for the starving in Somalia. Yet this solution did not have the intended impact. Examining environmental, political, and cultural processes helps us understand the complexity of this particular situation. Natural factors such as drought did lead to decreases in food production; however, "even in the years peace prevailed in Mogadishu, Somalia could never produce enough to feed its own people" (Biles 31). In addition, the flow of food in the country was intentionally impeded to foster the isolation of political opponents ("Hope behind the Horror" 41). Further, cultural divisions reinforced group definition and separation. For example, the Digil and Rahanwayn Somali clans were "socio-culturally and linguistically different" from the other four groups, which contributed to their being "politically and culturally subordinated" (Kusow 5). The result of these factors coming together was the dislocation and death of multitudes of Somalis.

Sending food did not and could not solve the food insecurity problem in Somalia. Even had the United States emptied its grain coffers and shipped enough food for all the hungry in such quantities to meet basic biological benchmarks, food insecurity would not have been eradicated. The famine was in part intentional as a means to acquire greater power in the country. Even had this aspect of the problem been resolved, food alone could not reconstruct a society in the context of Somalis as they defined themselves and their society rather than as refugees or inhabitants of feeding stations. The traditional approach would see the delivery of food as a short-run approach to tide the people over until growth could do its magic. The problem with this approach is that the same conditions that led to the famine are those that in large part intentionally destroyed and would continue to destroy the basis for traditionally defined economic growth. Solving food insecurity in Somalia required a redefinition of the food problem and the construction of a solution particular to the Somali context.

CONCLUSION

I began this chapter with the call from Catholic social teaching to make the fruits of the earth available to each individual, to dispose of the artificial impediments to all receiving what they need, and to remedy the tragedy of food insecurity in this world. Providing people with what they need is not simply a matter of offering greater accessibility; it requires a concerted effort to understand how the bounty of the earth is needed, desired, and utilized in different cultures and societies.

As difficult as the traditionally prescribed solutions to food insecurity may be to implement successfully, a more culturally appropriate approach is all the more difficult. It requires examination of food insecurity in each context from a different perspective. It requires humility in hearing the answers culturally different from one's own. It requires sacrifice, so that the toll of hunger might be stopped. And, at the start of a new millennium, it requires our response to God's call that we share the earth's bounty with all of creation.

WORKS CITED

Biles, Peter. "Anarchy." *Africa Report* (July–August 1992): 31–33.
Booth, Anne, and Syarifuddin Baharsyah. "Indonesia." In *Food*

Trade and Food Security in ASEAN and Australia, edited by Anne Booth, Cristinga C. David, et al., 1–36. Kuala Lampur and Canberra: ASEAN-Australia Joint Research Project, 1986.

Bread for the World Institute on Hunger and Development. *Hunger 1990: A Report on the State of World Hunger.* Washington, D.C.: Bread for the World Institute on Hunger and Development, 1990.

Cathie, John, and Dick Hermann. *Food Security and Macroeconomic Stabilization: A Case Study of Botswana, 1965–1984.* Tubingen: J. C. B. Mohr, 1987.

David, Christina C. "The Philippines." In *Food Trade and Food Security in ASEAN and Australia,* edited by Anne Booth, Cristinga C. David, et al., 85–116. Kuala Lampur and Canberra: ASEAN-Australia Joint Research Project, 1986.

Harris, Marvin. *Good to Eat.* New York: Simon and Schuster, 1985.

Herring, Ronald J. "The Dependent Welfare State: Nutrition, Entitlements, and Exchange in Sri Lanka." In *Pursuing Food Security: Strategies and Obstacles in Africa, Asia, Latin America, and the Middle East,* edited by W. Ladd Hollist and F. Lamond Tullis, 158–80. Boulder, Colo.: Lynne Rienner, 1987.

Hollist, W. Ladd. "The Politics of Hunger in Brazil." In *Pursuing Food Security: Strategies and Obstacles in Africa, Asia, Latin America, and the Middle East,* edited by W. Ladd Hollist and F. Lamond Tullis, 230–46. Boulder, Colo.: Lynne Rienner, 1987.

"Hope behind the Horror." *The Economist* 19 (June 1993): 41–42.

HungerSite. Available at: http://www.thehungersite.com.

John Paul II. *Centesimus Annus.* May 1, 1991.

Kusow, Abdi Mohamed. "Somalia's Silent Sufferers." *Africa News* 21 (December–January 1992–93): 5.

Leo XIII. *Rerum Novarum.* May 15, 1891.

Paul VI. *Populorum Progressio.* March 26, 1967.

World Bank. *Poverty and Hunger: Issues and Options for Food Security in Developing Countries.* Washington, D.C.: World Bank, 1986.

World Food Council. *Report of the World Food Council on the Work of Its Thirteenth Session, 15 June 1987.* Rome: World Food Council, 1987.

World Resources 1988–1989. New York: Basic, 1988.

FIVE

Contemporary Concerns

9

Liturgical Music at the Millennium

Timothy L. McDonald

A RECENT ISSUE of the journal *Pastoral Music* was entitled *Our Liturgical Century*. The main thesis of the issue was that there has been more liturgical change in the Catholic Church in the twentieth century than in any recent period. Likewise, music of the Catholic Church has undergone an enormous amount of change in the twentieth century. The purpose of this chapter is to examine briefly the documents and ideas that have helped to shape post–Vatican II liturgical music and to consider some of the issues that face composers, performers, and Catholic parishes in the year 2000 and beyond.

THE HERITAGE

Before considering the twentieth-century church documents relating to music, it is helpful to have an idea of the types of music used in Catholic liturgy in earlier centuries.

Plainchant is the sacred monophonic vocal music of the Church. Strongly influenced by Jewish sacred music, plainchant (also often called "plainsong" or simply "chant") employs a single, unaccompanied vocal line with a sacred Latin text. It is nonharmonic and nonrhythmic in nature. Although this music is often referred to as Gregorian chant in Catholic musical practice today, music historians point out that there are many repertories of chant, of which Gregorian is one. Other repertories of chant include Ambrosian (Milan), Mozarabic (Spain), Sarum (England), and Gallican (France).

Polyphony is a musical texture wherein multiple differing lines of music are employed simultaneously. No one is sure when sacred polyphony first developed. Writers make statements as early as the seventh century that can be interpreted as descriptions of polyphonic music, but the exact meaning of such statements is often unclear and can be explained in other ways. Polyphony was quite well developed by the late Middle Ages, but in the High and Late Renaissance the technique of imitative polyphony developed. This style of writing is characterized by multiple lines of music sounding simultaneously, with the beginning of each subsequent melodic line imitating the beginning of the first. The music is also composed a cappella ("in church style") or using voices with no instrumental accompaniment. All these elements can be seen in the music of Giovanni Pierluigi da Palestrina (c. 1525–94), one of the most successful of all composers to employ the style.

In 1749, an edict of Pope Benedict XIV approved the use of orchestrally accompanied music in church services, but in practice large-scale choral/orchestral works for liturgical use had been written since the mid–seventeenth century. In the late eighteenth century, some of the greatest musical works of all time were written in this form—the mass settings of composers such as Franz Joseph Haydn (1732–1809), Wolfgang Amadeus Mozart (1756–91), and Franz Peter Schubert (1797–1828).

The Cecilian Movement—named after St. Cecilia, patron saint of music—flourished in the nineteenth century and was still quite influential at the turn of the twentieth century. Cecilianism served as a reaction against orchestral/choral complexity and as a movement toward earlier styles that were considered purer, significantly plainchant and the Renaissance style of imitative polyphony. As extensions of this interest, the Solesmes monastic community produced better and more accurate editions of plainchant. Even composers who wrote at the turn of the twentieth century, such as Lorenzo Perosi (1872–1956), demonstrate a significant influence of chant and sixteenth-century polyphony in their music.

THE DOCUMENTS—FIRST HALF OF THE TWENTIETH CENTURY

Four documents published between 1903 and 1958 shed light on the Church's position regarding sacred music.

1. *Tra le Sollecitudini* (1903). Promulgated as a papal instruction from Pius X carrying the "force of law as a canonical code concerning sacred music," this document was issued as *"motu proprio et ex certa scientia"* on November 22 (significantly, the feast of St. Cecilia.). The document clearly identifies three types of music as appropriate for Catholic worship. Chant was clearly the most preferable style: "Gregorian chant . . . is . . . the proper chant of the Roman Church, the only chant which she has inherited from the ancient fathers, which she has jealously kept for so many centuries in her liturgical books . . . and which, lastly, has been so happily restored to its original perfection and purity by recent study" (qtd. in Joncas 13). The second type of music cited for inclusion in Catholic liturgy was Renaissance style polyphony:

> Music of the Classical school, especially . . . that of the Roman school, which reached its greatest perfection in the sixteenth century under [Giovanni] Pierluigi da Palestrina, and which afterwards went on producing excellent liturgical compositions . . . agrees well with the highest model of all sacred music, namely Gregorian chant, and therefore it deserves, together with Gregorian chant, to be used in the more solemn offices of the church. (qtd. in Joncas 14)

Modern music was certainly allowed, but Pius X displayed a reticence that illustrates his discomfort: "since modern music has become chiefly a secular art, greater care must be taken when admitting it, that nothing profane be allowed, nothing that is reminiscent of theatrical pieces, nothing based as to its form on the style of secular compositions" (qtd. in Joncas 14).

2. In *Mediator Dei* (1947), his major encyclical on the liturgy, Pius XII encouraged the Church "to promote with care congregational singing, and to see to its accurate execution with all due dignity, since it easily stirs up and arouses the faith and piety of large gatherings of the faithful" (qtd. in Winter 142). The strong emphasis on congregational singing foreshadows the concern that would be given this matter in the conciliar documents.

3. Pius XII issued the encyclical *Musicae Sacrae Disciplina* on Christmas Day 1955. The letter basically reaffirms the preference for chant and classical polyphony Pius X expressed in 1903. In addition, Pius XII gave support for modern composers who

write in a sixteenth-century style. The only real innovation is the identification of a fourth type of music considered appropriate for Catholic liturgy—the popular religious hymn. Note in the text of the following quote that although Pius XII mentions vernacular hymns and national or cultural differences, he does not perceive such hymns "intimately connected" to the liturgy:

> Besides those things that are intimately connected with the Church's sacred liturgy, there are also popular religious hymns which derive their origin from the liturgical chant itself. Most of these are written in the language of the people. Since those are closely related to the mentality and temperament of individual national groups, they differ considerably among themselves according to the character of different races and localities. (qtd. in Joncas 17)

4. *De Musica Sacra*, an "Instruction on Music and Liturgy," was published by the Sacred Congregation of Rites, an agency of the Curia. As an instructional document, it serves as a vehicle to show how existing legislation can be used in a practical manner. There is, however, one category of music it identifies that had not been previously recognized: instrumental sacred music, particularly organ music.

The Documents—Vatican II to the Late 1990s

Documents from the second half of the century vary from a conciliar constitution to statements by committees of American bishops to statements by composers themselves.

1. *Sacrosanctam Concilium* is known in English as *The Constitution on the Sacred Liturgy* and is one of the most important documents of Vatican II. Chapter 6 discusses sacred music. Important points addressed in this critical document are: *(a)* There is a need to preserve the "treasury of sacred music," including plainchant and classical polyphony. "The treasury of sacred music is to be preserved and fostered with great care. Choirs must be diligently promoted, especially in cathedrals" (*Sacrosanctam Concilium* 114, qtd. in Baum 53). *(b)* Chant is given primacy over other forms of sacred music. "The Church acknowledges Gregorian Chant as specially suited to the Roman liturgy; therefore, other

things being equal, it should be given pride of place in liturgical functions" (116). Clearly the authors of the document considered it critical that chant should be sung even in parishes with limited resources, for they included the following statement: "It is desirable also that an edition [of liturgical songbooks] be brought out containing simpler chants, for use in small churches" (117). (c) Other types of sacred music are acceptable. "But other kinds of sacred music, especially polyphony, are by no means excluded from liturgical celebrations, so long as they accord with the spirit of the liturgical action" (116). (d) Active participation of all the faithful is to be desired: "bishops and other pastors of souls must be at pains to insure [sic] that, whenever the sacred liturgy is to be solemnized with song, the whole body of the faithful may be able to contribute that active participation which is rightly theirs" (114). (e) Other styles of music, particularly those that represent traditions of different world cultures, can be appropriate liturgical music. "In certain parts of the world, especially in the mission lands, there are nations which have their own musical traditions, and these play a great part in their religious and social life. For this reason, due importance is to be attached to their music, and a suitable place is to be given to it, not only in forming their attitude toward religion, but also in adapting worship to their native genius" (119). (f) Musical texts should be biblical or liturgical. "The word-texts to be sung must always be in conformity with Catholic doctrine; indeed, they should be drawn chiefly from holy Scripture and from liturgical sources" (121).

2. *Musicam Sacram* was issued on March 5, 1967. Like the 1958 *De Musica Sacra*, it is an instruction released by an agency of the Curia—the Sacred Congregation for Divine Worship. It prescribes nothing new, but makes some assumptions: (a) Worshippers of the Roman Rite would take part in sung worship of both a Latin and a vernacular repertory, and (b) there is no problem with mixing Latin and vernacular texts in the same liturgy (Joncas 22–23).

3. *Music in Catholic Worship* (1972, revised 1983) and *Liturgical Music Today* (1982) were prepared by the Bishops' Committee on the Liturgy of the National Conference of Catholic Bishops. *Music in Catholic Worship* has been particularly influential in its

threefold manner of judging the value of music for the liturgy: (a) musical, (b) liturgical, and (c) pastoral.

Regarding musical judgment, the work asks, "Is the music technically, aesthetically, and expressively good? This judgment is basic and primary and should be made by competent musicians" (Funk 62). Liturgical judgment determines "what kind of music is called for, what parts are to be preferred for singing and who is to sing them" (63). Finally, a planning team or committee invokes pastoral judgment by the following question: "Does music in the celebration enable these people to express their faith, in this place, in this age, in this culture?" (65).

The authors of *Liturgical Music Today* identify it as an extension of *Music in Catholic Worship* and claim that it specifically addresses music in sacramental rites and the Liturgy of the Hours.

It is important to note that these works are documents of a conference of bishops in a particular country and not of the universal Church. Author John Huels, in *Liturgical Law: An Introduction*, comments on such statements:

> Diocesan bishops and conferences of bishops possess real authority over the liturgy and can enact legislation affecting the liturgy. . . . However, often the regulations they issue are not true laws because they are not promulgated as such. They appear as guidelines or pastoral directives. This does not mean that their observance is optional, but it indicates that the authority that issued them does not wish to have the same "weight" that the law itself possesses. (qtd. in Joncas 7)

4. "The Milwaukee Report" (1992) and "The Snowbird Statement" (1995) come from composers and performers rather than from church officials, yet they represent perhaps the best picture of some of the main issues and controversies at the millennium.

Archbishop Rembert Weakland, O.S.B., organized and hosted five meetings between 1982 and 1992 called the Milwaukee Symposia for Church Composers. "The Milwaukee Symposia for Church Composers: A Ten-Year Report" (better known by its abbreviated title—"The Milwaukee Report") is critical of some elements of both the *Constitution on the Sacred Liturgy* from Vatican II and *Music in Catholic Worship*. Its strongest suggestions relate to the relationship of music to ritual, and the need for cross-cultural music making.

"The Snowbird Statement on Catholic Liturgical Music" (better known by its abbreviated title—"The Snowbird Statement") is the result of meetings held in Snowbird and Salt Lake City, Utah, in 1992 and 1993. The seventeen signers of the document are primarily musicians from large churches and cathedrals, although several are primarily academics. The statement was issued on November 1, 1995, and differs quite remarkably from "The Milwaukee Report." As Father Jan Michael Joncas (a theologian, composer, and performer who is also a participant in the Milwaukee Symposia) points out, some consider "The Snowbird Statement" to be a rejoinder to "The Milwaukee Report" (Joncas 9).

ISSUES IN SACRED MUSIC AT THE MILLENNIUM

"The Milwaukee Report" and "The Snowbird Statement" reflect very different approaches to liturgical music among performers and composers. Among the central issues are musical style, the concepts of quality and beauty, technical training for musicians, and ways to address the pluralism of cultures that is becoming more and more representative of multicultural America.

Musical Styles

At the most basic level, those responsible for choosing liturgical music must ask what type of music should be used in services. If the basis for decision is to be the documents cited above, then one matter to consider is the virtual absence of chant and classical polyphony in most churches.

Even if we are to discount the documents written before Vatican II, virtually all other documents cite the importance of this repertory. As noted previously, its importance was clearly cited in *The Constitution on the Sacred Liturgy*, even to the extent of the directive that chant be given "pride of place in liturgical functions." Even the U.S. bishops address the issue in *Music in Catholic Worship*: "[Musicians] must also do the research needed to find new uses for the best of the old music. . . . They must find practical means of preserving and using our rich heritage of

Latin chants and motets" (Funk 62). Although the same document gives support for other styles, it is unequivocal in its support for the traditional music of the church:

> Good music of new styles is finding a happy home in the celebrations of today. To chant and polyphony we have effectively added the chorale hymn, restored responsorial singing to some extent, and employed many styles of contemporary composition. Music in folk idiom is finding acceptance in eucharistic celebrations. We must judge value within each style. (Funk 62)

Edward Foley and Mary McGann, in a particularly concise and well-written account of the development of American Catholic liturgical music after Vatican II, suggest some reasons for the disappearance of chant: (1) Latin and English have different accents; (2) chant was associated with a pre–Vatican II concept of worship, "whose transformation by the Council presumed a parallel musical transformation as well"; and (3) the complexity of chant was intended for monks and trained specialists, and it "did not recommend itself to large-scale performance by ordinary congregations" (Foley and McGann 2).

Although there is no doubt an element of truth in what Foley and McGann say, some of their comments are questionable. For example, the comment about the council's presumption of a parallel musical transformation directly contradicts the previously cited statements from *The Constitution on the Sacred Liturgy* regarding chant and polyphony. Furthermore, although I would not dispute the complexity of chant, anyone who has heard the strong, powerful response of many congregations to the chanted "Our Father" knows that a fairly intricate chant can be mastered technically and become a powerful element in a liturgical celebration.

I believe we must look elsewhere for a reason for the disappearance of chant, and Foley and McGann have identified it:

> A second development in American Roman Catholic music centered around the growing desire for a more popular musical style in our worship song. The experience of celebrating the liturgy in English was an important impetus to the widening search for a sound that was identifiably "American." In this process many composers turned to the gospel and the folk-rock idioms which governed the popular music scene at that time. (3)

It does not seem difficult to me to justify the use of popular styles of music liturgically. *Musicam Sacram* of 1967 allowed for other styles of music in parts of the world where such styles formed an important part of the cultural and social life. One could certainly claim that the importance of popular music in American cultural life would logically lead to its inclusion in liturgical music. Furthermore, the "pastoral judgment" that is such an important factor in *Music in Catholic Worship* also supports the inclusion of popular styles because this style of music in our age and culture does indeed help people to express their faith.

However, I would argue that the "treasury of sacred music" the conciliar authors and the American bishops have identified is not being preserved today. Jan Michael Joncas supports this belief:

> in spite of the exhortations of *S[acrosanctam] C[oncilium]* and the post–Vatican II implementation documents, the treasury of sacred music consisting of Gregorian chant, Ars Nova and Renaissance polyphony, Baroque, Classical and Romantic Masses, Requiems, and motets has almost completely disappeared from Rome [*sic*] Rite worship. Concentrated efforts must be engaged if elements of this repertoire are to be retained in Roman Rite worship as living prayer rather than museum curiosities. (Joncas 113)

Quality of Music

An area of much discussion and dissension in recent years has to do with the quality of music that is performed. The U.S. bishops were aware of the issue in 1972 and 1983 when they wrote in *Music in Catholic Worship* that "Only artistically sound music will be effective in the long run. To admit the cheap, the trite, the musical cliché often found in popular songs for the purpose of 'instant liturgy' is to cheapen the liturgy, to expose it to ridicule, and to invite failure" (Funk 62).

One of the problems, of course, is the manner in which quality is assessed. One way that would seem appropriate is to use the tools of music theory. This discipline has been used for centuries and is still being used to analyze and to compose music. Although music theory (and its related subdisciplines of harmony, counterpoint, and analysis) has primarily focused on classical styles of music, most forms of popular music utilize the same basic chord structures. In fact, popular styles adhere much more to traditional theory than many classical styles in the twentieth century. A special branch of music theory called jazz theory has developed over the years to deal with the special nature (and the often more complex chords) of that style.

In a section entitled "Cross-Cultural Music Making," "The Milwaukee Report" employs very strong language regarding this issue:

> The development of common-practice procedures in tonal music that eventually crystallized into compositional rules in the West further upholds the superiority of the style of composition flourishing in Northern Europe from the seventeenth to the nineteenth centuries. This Bach-Beethoven-Brahms paradigm is consistently employed as the standard by which all other composition—including worship music—must be judged. ("Milwaukee Symposia" 35–36)

The report takes an even stronger position in the following quote:

> From a musical perspective, accepting the challenge of cross-cultural worship requires addressing the ethnocentrism that has marked Western Christian music for the last millennium. While in times past there may have been good reasons for upholding Gregorian Chant and the music of Palestrina as the best models of Christian ritual music, the continuation of such assertions carries the cultural message that medieval and Renaissance music of Western Europe is somehow intrinsically better than music of other eras or other cultures. ("Milwaukee Symposia" 35)

There are some problems with these statements. In the first place, many other styles of music utilize the theoretical and harmonic systems that "Milwaukee" associates with either northern or western Europe. Geographically, one could include South Africa, parts of South America, Australia, and North America (not to mention central, eastern, and southern Europe, which are curiously omitted).

Even more disturbing is the charge of ethnocentrism from the signers of the document because many of them compose in a popular style, and, as I pointed out before, popular music uses basically the same harmonic system. Is it ethnocentric to use the system in classical styles but not in popular styles?

It also seems hypocritical for the signers themselves to make a charge of ethnocentrism in a section on cross-culturalism. As an astute respondent noted, "the composers of the 'reformed-folk' idiom, who were the primary authors of the report, are overwhelmingly white and male. Their musical style is not cross-cultural, it is merely a pale imitation of popular 'soft rock' " (Townley 5).

Finally, if assessing a special value to traditional music of the Catholic Church is ethnocentric, then we must assume that when pious Lutherans or Methodists sing some of the wonderful traditional hymns from their faith traditions, they, too, are displaying ethnocentrism.

The strongest points made by "The Snowbird Statement" relate to beauty, quality, and the need for education and formation of liturgical musicians. The authors of the document mention beauty early on: "We believe that beauty is essential in the liturgical life and mission of the church. Beauty is an effective—even sacramental—sign of God's presence and action in the world. . . . An injustice is committed against God's people when styles of worship and liturgical art are promoted which lack aesthetic beauty" ("Snowbird Statement" 13).

Next, the authors address the issue of quality:

> We wish to affirm standards of excellence in the composition and performance of all musical forms in the church's liturgy: congregational, choral, cantorial, diaconal, presidential and instrumental. There is no necessary inconsistency between traditional standards of excellence and the pastoral principles of the renewed liturgy; nor does sound liturgical theology suggest such a discrepancy. Where standards of excellence exist in theory or in practice they should be sustained; where they do not exist they should be developed and fostered. (14)

At this point, however, the most divisive issue surfaces when the authors of "Snowbird" assert that "some music is of higher quality than others; not all music is good" (15). Although musical standards change, nevertheless "the elements that comprise the musical judgment are objective and are more than mere assertions of personal preference or of historical or social convention" (15).

The authors address and clearly reject relativism. They suggest that comparisons and decisions regarding quality can be made, even among different styles of music, because "to the extent that many of the styles employed in English-language Catholic worship today are dialects of the same larger musical language (in terms of harmonic vocabulary or rhythmic organization), a discussion of musical quality across stylistic boundaries is valid and necessary" (15).

The authors suggest that there is "a characteristic ethos of Catholic liturgical music . . . discernable, for instance, in music that elaborates the sacramental mysteries in a manner attentive to the public, cosmic and transcendent character of religion, rather than in styles of music that are overly personalized, introverted or privatized" (15). (Thomas Day refers to this focus as "Ego Renewal" in his work *Why Catholics Can't Sing: The Culture of Catholicism and the Triumph of Bad Taste* [51].)

Finally, the authors of "The Snowbird Statement" state that music that would embody this ethos of music is not limited to any particular type of composition or specific period of time. However, "music employed by countless generations of Catholic Christians is the starting point for discerning the characteristics of a Catholic ethos in liturgical music." They believe that new styles of music will develop because of the new cultural contexts in which the church worships. "This process of development, however, should consult pre-existing forms to a greater extent than has generally been the case in recent decades. We advocate that new forms and styles grow organically from extant forms which display a Catholic ethos. We seek to articulate more objectively the characteristics of the Catholic ethos which we intuitively believe to exist" (15). Not surprisingly, a response to "Snowbird" criticized this statement. "This sounds a bit like the Supreme Court Justice on pornography: It can't be defined, but you'll recognize it when you see it. Even so, the same issue of recognition and definition is at stake because the question has to do with 'good' music for liturgy. Who decides?" (Gallen 21).

In a fascinating article, Thomas Day examined the issue of

quality and style in the framework of artistic modernism and postmodernism. As he describes it, modernism suggests that "the art of the past, that is, whatever is not designated as modern and 'serious,' would be preserved as museum pieces, but it was essentially exhausted, spiritually sterile, aesthetically boring, and had no more to offer." By contrast, postmodernism has "many meanings, one of which is that the old and the new have a lot to offer each together and can coexist in a mutually beneficial tension" ("What's Happening" 41).

Day suggests that after Vatican II the Church entered its own phase of artistic modernism, with an optimistic belief that the new music (especially "folk" music) would bring great progress for the Church. "Out went the pipe organ. Out went the choir. The song-of-the-week by the composer-of-the-week was the supposed vehicle for transporting us to this glorious future." A postmodernist reaction ensued, and the choir and some traditional music returned. Reaction was followed by counterreaction when some experts proclaimed that traditional works distorted the intentions of Vatican II ("What's Happening" 41).

It is in this context that "The Milwaukee Report" and "The Snowbird Statement" are to be placed, according to Day. "Milwaukee" is an attempt at a compromise between artistic modernism and postmodernism, and "Snowbird" is an assertion that all is not well. Day also suggests that

> for all its good intentions, the same document unwittingly reinforces the status quo and asserts once again the unquestioned authority of modernism: 1) Whenever the *Report* mentions classic liturgical music (for example, chant) the surrounding context is always slightly negative and full of cautionary language; 2) the *Report* unintentionally created a new "White List" of approved composers and liturgists. . . . *The Milwaukee Report* was put together mostly by "insiders" who have created their own world to be "inside" of. . . . *The Snowbird Statement* was written mostly by people who are, despite their notable accomplishments and the prestige of their jobs, "outsiders." ("What's Happening" 41–42)

There is some evidence to suggest that Day is correct regarding the insider/outsider matter. He is certainly correct in his claim that in journals such as *Pastoral Music* the prose writings of the "insiders" are quoted authoritatively. In fact, it is enlightening to compare the two issues of the journal in which the reports were printed. "The Milwaukee Report" appeared in larger than standard print, and the cover title clearly identified it as the main focus of that issue of *Pastoral Music* ("Why Catholics Sing: The 'Milwaukee Report' "). Furthermore, the editor, Father Virgil Funk, discusses the report in his introduction ("In this issue"). By contrast, when "The Snowbird Statement" was printed in the same journal, it received standard print size and had no mention either on the cover or in the editor's comments.

SUMMARY

Two major issues facing musicians and liturgists in the year 2000 and beyond are: (1) What do we sing? and (2) How do we select music and assess its value?

Regarding what we sing, we are clearly not following the instructions of the conciliar and postconciliar documents. As we have seen, chant and classical polyphony are regarded as treasures of the Church. *The Constitution on the Sacred Liturgy* describes chant as having "pride of place in liturgical functions," and in *Music in Catholic Worship* the U.S. bishops instructed pastoral musicians to "find practical means of preserving and using our rich heritage of Latin chants and motets." This is clearly not happening to the extent intended in most U.S. parishes.

There is certainly a need for a variety of styles and cultures in American liturgical music. Popular styles are obviously an important part of American secular culture and can serve to inspire worshipers and bring them closer to God. Popular styles change rapidly, however, and can appear dated and even open to ridicule. Consider the fate of some of the "folk" repertory from the early post–Vatican II era.

We need to assess the impact of commercialization on music of the Church. Major publishers such as Oregon Catholic Press and GIA Music have a great deal at stake financially by promoting sales of music and recordings of liturgical and devotional music. It is likely that revenues from sales of popular styles of music are greater than those from sales of more traditional styles. Even within popular styles, wouldn't a poor or mediocre work from an established composer be more likely to be published than a good composition by an unknown writer? The role of publishers was a recurrent theme at a series of presentations called "Church Music 2000" at the annual convention of the National Association of Pastoral Musicians in Pittsburgh in July 1999.

We must pursue the issue of quality in assessing liturgical music. *Music in Catholic Worship* identifies the "musical judgement" as an important element in this determination and calls for competent musicians to make such decisions. "The Milwaukee Report" correctly points out that the musical, liturgical, and pastoral judgments cannot be made separately, but must be made together. Musical parameters—largely based on an inclusive music theory that includes popular, jazz, and multicultural styles—must enter the discussion.

Finally, if Catholic Church music is to be truly "catholic"—that is, "universal"—we must include more than popular styles in our liturgy. There is a place for music from other cultures, including that of our Catholic past.

WORKS CITED

Baum, Gregory, ed. *The Teachings of the Second Vatican Council: Complete Texts of the Constitutions, Decrees, and Declarations.* Westminster, Md.: Newman, 1966.

Day, Thomas, "What's Happening to *Pastoral Music?*" *Pastoral Music* 21, no. 3 (February–March 1997): 41–44.

———. *Why Catholics Can't Sing: The Culture of Catholicism and the Triumph of Bad Taste.* New York: Crossroad, 1988.

Foley, Edward, and Mary McGann. *Music and the Eucharistic Prayer.* Collegeville, Minn.: Liturgical, 1988.

Funk, Virgil C., ed. *Music in Catholic Worship.* Rev. ed.. The NPM commentary. Washington, D.C.: Pastoral, 1983.

Gallen, John. "Engaged Melody: A Paradigm for Liturgy." *Pastoral Music* 20, no. 5 (June–July 1996): 21–23.

Joncas, Jan Michael. *From Sacred Song to Ritual Music: Twentieth-*

Century Understandings of Roman Catholic Worship Music. Collegeville, Minn.: Liturgical, 1997.

"The Milwaukee Symposia for Church Composers: A Ten-Year Report." *Pastoral Music* 17, no. 1 (October–November 1992): 19–50.

"The Snowbird Statement on Catholic Liturgical Music." *Pastoral Music* 20, no. 3 (February–March 1996): 13–19.

Townley, Richard. "Milwaukee Report: 'Reformed-Folk' Perspective" (letter to the editor). *Pastoral Music* 18, no. 4 (April–May 1993): 5.

Winter, Miriam Therese. *Why Sing? Toward a Theology of Catholic Church Music*. Washington, D.C.: Pastoral, 1984.

10

Evolution, Creationism, and Catholicism at the Millennium

Richard E. Wilson

INTRODUCTION

I MUST RUSH TO explain that I undertook to write this little treatise in order to refresh and reorganize my own thinking on the questions of evolution and creationism at the end of the twentieth century. I am no great seer, so my perspective on the next millennium is severely limited. But I do have a good understanding, I believe, of the nature of science and scientific thought and an inherent trust that as *Homo sapiens* (the modern human) continues to evolve, though the thoughts and understandings of nature will become better and more sophisticated, the process of how men and women (both in and out of science) think will remain essentially the same. The thought processes of science are extraordinarily creative, and that will not change in the next millennium. I do hope, however, that humankind will become more ecologically and evolutionarily aware and conservative in the next millennium.

As we ended the twentieth century, the controversy in the United States regarding evolution and creationism was as vocal as it was at the turn of the nineteenth century. The major difference is that today the argument is largely restricted to the United States, whereas at the end of the nineteenth century it was a western European and American discussion. The vociferous nonacceptance of evolution as a scientific theory with reality and scope as broad as the theories involving gravitation, genes, and plate tectonics is limited singularly to a small number of American fundamentalist or evangelical Christian religions (a small number of religions, but an inordinately large portion of the population, particularly in the traditional Bible Belt). The rest of the educated world is no longer engaged in the argument. Though this is a truism, the argument grows louder in the United States, not softer. Witness the recent Kansas Board of Education vote to let local school boards decide whether to teach or not to teach evolution—boards that are subject to local prejudices rather than open to an appreciation of the broad acceptance of the science of evolution. What societal and intellectual events have allowed this situation, and are they likely to persist into the next century?

More than forty years ago, C. P. Snow bemoaned that there was a fragmentation of knowledge causing a growth of "two cultures" in Western society. He was referring primarily to the fact that scholars in science and those in the arts were growing apart in both what they thought and how they thought about it. Many observers would argue that since then even more fragmentation has occurred. As we look to the next millennium, will this trend continue? And whose fault is it, the scientist's or the nonscientist's?

J. A. Breyer, in an editorial, notes that "many artists and intellectuals scorn science as mere fact and observation, as unfeeling and unemotional, a passionless activity practiced by beings who have sacrificed their humanity on the altars of objectivity and reproducible results" (150). He argues that it is the fault of the modern scientists because we teach science as a "battery of techniques" not as a drama of ideas. He further argues "the evolution of ideas is more important than advances in technology" (150). Science is and should be a very human activity, and we need to be sure that is more apparent to students rather than less!

Jacob Bronowski argues that the truth of science is not the truth of facts, but the truth of the laws and concepts that bring unity to those facts. He says,

> Truth in science is like Everest, an ordering of the facts. We organize our experience in patterns which, formalized, make the

network of scientific laws. But science does not stop at the formulation of laws; we none of us do, and none of us, in public with his work or in private with his conscience, lives by following a schedule of laws. So science takes its coherence, its intellectual and imaginative strength together, from the concepts at which its laws cross, like knots in a mesh. Gravitation, mass and energy, evolution, enzymes, the gene and the unconscious—there are the bold creations of science, the strong invisible skeleton on which it articulates the movements of the world. (52)

Albert Einstein once noted that "the most incomprehensible thing about the universe is that it is comprehensible." From the creation myths of the first humans to the most esoteric modern theory of strings, humans have sought to comprehend the universe. This desire to know, to understand the universe and our place in it, is a very human trait. We all seek truth, whether it is the truth of the heart, the truth of the mind, the truth of emotions, or the truth of the intellect, and truth unites us and should not divide us as intellects. This fusion of intellectual common ground should (and must!) persist into the next millennium.

Crucial to the evolution-creation debate is most fundamentalists' clear lack of understanding of the nature of science. Ludwick Fleck, a sociologist of science, notes among other things that the scientific method is not a set sequence of things to do, but rather the way scientists think. He makes very clear that no bare scientific fact exists. Rather, he notes that facts develop slowly and in a specific historical ambience. The facts represent and make known views of what Fleck identifies as "the thought collective," those scientists who share a "thought style" or joint system of viewing the world (41).

Lynn Margulis, in discussing Fleck, says that

New scientific knowledge makes its formal debut in any professional journal as statements tentative, peculiar and often esoteric even to co-authors. The creative act of members of the thought collective is to organize, edit, and reshape the primary science accordingly. Fellow scientists imbue scientific pronouncements with authority and present them for members of their thought collective as textbook truth. But even a clearly stated new scientific fact is usually met with resistance by the collective, resistance that is eventually overcome and ultimately consolidated into an interlocking system of consistent ideas that, taken together, are comprehensible as part of a newly emerging thought style. (viii)

Scientists accept as fact only that which the scientific process has reviewed and received over time. And even then, they feel free to reinvestigate and revalidate the fact, for that is what science is about!

On the proposition at hand, evolution versus creationism, I think Fleck shed immense light. He writes,

> Truth is not "relative" and certainly not "subjective" in the popular sense of the word. It is always, or almost always determined with a thought style. One can never say that the same thought is true for A and false for B. For if they [people A and B] belong to the same thought collective, the thought will either be true or false for both. But if they belong to different thought collectives, it will just not be the same thought! It must be unclear to, or be understood differently, by one of them. Truth is not a convention, *but rather (1) in historical perspective, an event in the history of thought, (2) in its contemporary context, stylized thought constraint.* (100, italics in original)

All ideas in science, including evolution, have progressed from early, simple notions to more complex concepts, and all have undergone the scrutiny of the thought collective.

Charles Darwin's proposition that we humans evolved from an ancestor of the ape family now offends only a limited group of people, the religious fundamentalists and the uneducated. Interestingly, the corollary that humans are consequently typical primates and entirely driven by their peculiar genetic heritage seems to offend almost everybody. As R. Morrison notes,

> People accept that the genes are the sole driving force for animals because animals are just that, mere animals. By contrast they say, we humans are unique in that we possess both a spiritual and intellectual capacity separate from and independent of our physical body. Consequently there is consensus across all cultures that this independence of mind bestows both a unique sense of self-awareness and the ability, and even responsibility, to tailor our behavior to fit the dictates of reason and countermand what are the baser instincts of our animal heritage. (xii)

As the new millennium dawns, the human genome project is elucidating ever more clearly what our heritage is. Carl Sagan and others proposed that the classification of humans as a separate family Hominidae, a family distinct from the great apes, is untenable in the light of DNA studies. They would argue that we should be properly placed within the chimpanzee family (Pongidae) and genus *(Pan)*. It has been often said that we humans share 98.4 percent of our total DNA with the chimps, but at least 95 percent of that is so called "nonsense" DNA, vast stretches of repeating base pairs that code for nothing. If we look at the active, coding portions of the DNA, we find that there is a 99.6 percent match (Sagan and Druyan 276). Surely a mere 0.4 percent difference between us and *Pan paniscus* (the bonobo or pygmy chimpanzee) has to be seen as significant.

With this perspective, let us look at the historical discussions of evolution and try to glean if the thought collective has operated well. And if it has, I need not be a "seer" (as I noted above), but should be able to forecast the future of evolution, creationism, and the Catholic Church in the next millennium.

What Darwin Said

Charles Darwin wrote *Origin of Species* in 1859. We should rush to note that the concept of evolution was around and actively being discussed all through the eighteenth and nineteenth centuries. What Darwin's book really set out to do was to provide the first and most viable mechanism that could be accepted on a scientific basis for explaining what a large part of the scientific community already believed was probable. Even more to the point, Darwin himself rarely used the term *evolution* because he felt that the word as used in England and Europe inferred a vision of progressiveness, of one thing leading inevitably to something improved or better. In fact, the full title of Darwin's most notable treatise was *The Origin of Species by Means of Natural Selection* or *The Preservation of Favoured Races in the Struggle for Life.* The full title speaks to his desire only to provide a mechanism. He himself always used the term *descent by modification* rather than *evolution*.

So his point was that species change, and new species come into existence—not as most of his critics think by species B succeeding species A because species B is an improved and better version of A (evolution as progressive), but rather because at least some individuals from species A become modified by natural processes and now exist and are reproductively isolated from species B. Additionally some forms of species A may and most likely continue to exist after species B has come into existence. Darwin didn't see this as "progress forward" but rather simply change over time, which does not necessarily produce an improved version of species A.

Darwin got his ideas from many sources, not the least of which was Thomas Malthus (1798). Malthus was an economist who wrote *An Essay on the Principle of Population.* In talking about the sudden surge occurring in the world's populations, he argued that populations grew geometrically (almost logarithmically) while food supplies grew arithmetically. The resultant was that soon populations would outstrip their food resources, and many individuals would die because of starvation. Darwin saw in that notion the basic mechanism he needed for his idea of how evolution would occur. As proposed by Darwin, natural selection says that there are many more individuals born than survive; those that survive in some way must have been favored, whereas those that die off are selected against by limiting factors, such as food or space or ability to withstand environmental conditions or whatever factor might be operating at that moment. Darwin then proposed that the population of individuals that survived must be somehow "modified" or different from their predecessors. In modern terms, we now know that they must be different genetically, with individuals that carry certain genes having been eliminated, leaving behind a population that has a somewhat different genetic makeup.

According to Darwin's logic, succeeding populations may or may not be "better" in any cosmic or universal sense, just different. Furthermore, the potential fate of the species is the same as was the fate of its predecessor—namely, that if it is suitable to the conditions, it will survive and persist, and if it is not suitable, it will go to extinction or at least undergo modification again. Incidentally, though this concept has come to be called "survival of the fittest," that phrase was coined by the philosopher Spencer and not used by Darwin until a later edition of *Origin.*

There were two further premises of Darwin's concept of natural selection—namely, that there must be a mechanism by which this change in biological makeup must be passed on (today we know this to be genetics-DNA) and that all populations show a great degree of variation. It is important to note on the first issue that the science of genetics did not exist in Darwin's time. Gregor Mendel, the father of genetics, was working on his sweet peas in an Austrian monastery in the 1850s, but there is no evidence that he and Darwin corresponded, and all of Mendel's work lay unknown until the early 1900s, when Robert de Vries rediscovered it (Darwin died in 1881). So Darwin actually could not explain inheritability (though he had a theory), but he was confident that it was necessary, and he actually did a number of experiments with pigeons and domesticated animals and plants to demonstrate it. But he, along with all naturalists of the time, believed that parents contributed something to shape and give characteristics to the next generation.

On the latter issue, high variation, Darwin had extensive examples from his five-year voyage on the *HMS Beagle* and from extensive studies he did on barnacles and pigeons. His simplest argument was to ask one to look at humans and the variation seen there. So the core ideas of natural selection were (1) more organisms are born than can possibly survive, (2) characteristics must be inherited, and (3) all populations have a degree of variation.

How then did these seemingly simple ideas become what many have described the single greatest novel idea of the nineteenth century (and perhaps the twentieth) and lead to the broiling controversy around us, as recently as the Kansas Board of Education's decision last fall to take evolution out of the science standards and make teaching it optional to the local school districts? It is very important to note the fundamental significance of Darwin's ideas: evolution is the core of all modern biology, and the basic ideas expressed above are still the basis in fact for our belief in evolution as biologists. The details have been hugely expanded, and many subsets of the basic idea have been expressed, but to their core all modern biologists consider the three basic premises to be valid and indisputable. The thought collective has taken Darwin's ideas, critiqued, and edited them to give us the modern theory that, though more elaborate, is still basic Darwinism.

So why then the problems? If we stick just with the biology, Victorian England had some problems at first because Darwinism seemed to run contrary to the tenets of the Anglican Church. Particularly, when in 1871 Darwin published *The Descent of Man, and Selection in Relation to Sex*, religious (and political) conservatives were upset. This book suggested that humans, too, had come to be by means of natural selection, specifically by descent from apes. To any literal readers of the Bible, this idea contradicted the Genesis account of creation. Note that there are, at this point in history, two thought collectives considering one problem, from two different histories and thought processes!

On a broader scale, Darwinism almost took on a life of its own. Many authors now tried to take the basic principle of survival of the fittest and apply it all parts of life. The colonial period of Western history was in full flower in the late 1800s, and what better explanation available for white Europeans to be able to control world trade, particularly the African and Asian subcontinents, than "We white Europeans are the fittest, so we control all the wealth and you all work for us"? In the United States, Darwinism was applied broadly to economics with the robber barons "deserving" their great wealth because, according to good Keynesian economics, he who was most fit should grow rich. Darwinism was even added to the original ideas of Marx and Engels in *Manifesto on Communism* (1848), which Engels revised in English in 1888. Darwinism was used as justification for all people being unified for the greater good, the even distribution of all goods and wealth under communism, and as a way to prevent and protect less-fit humans from being eliminated or exploited. Though this may seem a digression, sometimes in looking only at the current discussion, we forget what has colored the arguments for one hundred years and perhaps influenced the thought collectives on each side of the debate.

The Current Controversy and the Understanding of Science

Having given a brief look at Darwinism, evolution, and its basic premises, let us now turn to the modern discourse. The discussions in Kansas, Texas, and in parts of California and Georgia are particularly troubling because they have moved away from the arena of healthy intellectual debate and have become wars of words and almost sinister retribution. Particularly in some of the fundamentalist and somewhat uniquely American Christian churches, to believe in evolution is to be *godless* and *satanic*, words that have been applied to many who teach evolution. The conservative movement of American politics in the past twenty years has also fueled the debate, and often it is difficult to find a firm line between what is political debate and what is religion-driven debate. Despite our constitutional injunction for the separation of church and state, the lines are currently somewhat murky. Whether you agree with my assessment or not, we do have a vocal, antievolution debate going on in this country. Will this debate, or should it, persist into the next millennium?

In order to address the problem and gaze efficiently into the crystal ball, let us add clarity on one other element of the debate. Having discussed the tenets of evolution and natural selection, we should consider the following question: What is the nature of science? This question is necessary in order to be sure we are all operating from the same paradigm. The central arguments between evolution and creationism, in the hands of intelligent people, become at least less vitriolic if we can establish what science really is.

Science is a way of thinking; it is an orderly approach to discovering the ways of nature. When following the scientific method, a scientist sees something around him/her about which he/she wishes to ask a question; the scientist then proposes a hypothesis, a reasonable explanation of the phenomena observed; the scientist then performs an experiment to test that hypothesis, and from that experiment either falsifies or defeats the hypothesis or sustains that at least under those test conditions the hypothesis appears to be true. The scientist now forms a theory, which stands as the scientific explanation for the natural phenomena, until such time as another scientist comes along and challenges and tests the theory and finds it wanting. The scientist seeks proximate truth, but the real joy of good science is to make refinements and continue to strengthen our understanding. Science rarely achieves final truth; that is, *science does not prove anything!*

Given that is what science is, science cannot test everything. It is limited by its current technology and the human being's creative intellect. Might we be able to test something scientifically one hundred years from now that we currently can't test? Sure! But science can never scrutinize a multitude of human mental phenomena, including ideas such as beauty, love, God (or the primary cause). If we cannot subject an idea or concept to tests, we cannot approach that idea scientifically. Some believe that a picture such as the *Mona Lisa* is beautiful and exquisite art. I personally believe that some of Leonardo da Vinci's drawings of helicopters are inherently better art. Can I subject to science your belief that the *Mona Lisa* is great art? Well, I guess I could do a survey of three thousand people asking them if the *Mona Lisa* is great art. If I were doing good inferential science, they would all have to be equally uneducated and unexposed to discussions of great art. At best, I might say, "because 2,345 people of 3,000 think the *Mona Lisa* is great art, it probably is." I will not have demonstrated that it was great art, rather only that 78 percent of the people polled think the *Mona Lisa* is great art.

We take paradigms such as beauty, love, and God on what I like to call our human "faith" systems. We believe with all our heart that the tree blooming outside today is beautiful, that my significant others love me, or even that I love them. Scientists, too, can hold to their faith systems when they love, believe in God, or appreciate great beauty. The important fact is that good scientists recognize when they are being scientists and when they are in their belief systems. Science cannot be taken on faith, and faith is not science!

Lest you think we have really wandered way afield, let us finally come back to what is the problem between evolution and creationism. The central issue is that evolution is a valid scientific theory, and natural selection as its chief mechanism is absolutely verifiable by scientific means. Creationism is not verifiable scientifically because it centers on a belief in God as the creator. Most evolutionists I know believe in God, but when they do, they are in their belief systems, not their science. Stephen Hawking's description of the origin of the universe from a single "big bang" is still very much a theory, but daily physicists test various aspects of it through what they perceive are its manifestations in novas and the like. Are these godless people? Oddly enough, no one panned the fine movie *Contact* of a couple years ago, starring Jody Foster, as ridiculous because scientists were looking for life on other planets. Most of those physicists believe in God, believing at some point that there is/was a "first cause." But as scientists they don't hold to the folly that they can place God at some exact point; rather, they choose to believe in God, but scientifically test the nature provided by that God to try to come to understanding natural phenomena. As Einstein said, "the most incomprehensible thing about the universe is that it is comprehensible"!

If one considers the controversy carefully, the evolution-creation debate is really one of science and religion. And if we can put it in that context, it becomes a much less rancorous debate because then we don't have the ego-invested problem of having to contemplate the horrible likelihood of having descended from apes, species we are eliminating in our ecological stupidity. The real ignorance of the current debate in Kansas and elsewhere is that those who dismiss evolution as "just a theory" and charge that the people who subscribe to it and investigate it are godless and satanic are saying in essence that it is wrong to investigate any observable natural phenomena lest we discover something new. Though most of them don't realize it, they are really rejecting science. Or to be religious about it, they are suggesting that in looking carefully at the laws of nature as scientists, we might just discover something more about God, which might be unnerving to our long-existing religious paradigms!

History Repeats Itself

A new book about Galileo entitled *Galileo's Daughter*, by Dava Sobel (1999), is a wonderful "memoir of science, faith, and love" (the book's subtitle). The parallels between the Catholic Church's condemnation of Galileo because he supported the Copernican theory that the earth traveled around the Sun instead of the old Ptolemaic theory that the earth was the center of the universe and the current debate between segments of Christianity and evolution are almost frightening. History has taught us nothing, and we are fated to repeat the same stupidity that finally led to Pope John Paul II's apology in 1992 for the Galileo affair, 359 years later.

The Galileo story illuminates my point about science versus faith systems and may give us some insight into Catholicism in the next millennium. Galileo Galilei was born in 1564 and died in 1642 at the ripe old age of seventy-eight. He was the son of a musician and at ten went to study at a Benedictine monastery, but when he was about to become a novice, his father withdrew him because the father would have had to bear Galileo's expenses, which he neither could afford nor wished to afford. By 1610, Galileo had invented the telescope, had gained international fame across all of Europe, and was the "Chief Mathematician of the University of Pisa and Philosopher and Mathematician" to the grand duke of Tuscany, Don Cosimo de' Medici, a position he basically held the rest of his life. Though Galileo tutored individually many aristocratic students, including some who ultimately sat in judgment on him in 1633, he was relieved from any daily or yearly teaching duties at Pisa. His most important astronomical discovery was to find the four moons of Jupiter with his new instrument.

Galileo had written some books on gravity and motion, which set the stage for Newton at the end of the 1600s. But in 1610, he wrote a major treatise entitled *The Starry Messenger*, which he dedicated to the young duke, his benefactor, Cosimo II. Within one week of publication, the 550 copies printed had sold out as news of its contents spread rapidly. This work ultimately led to the discovery, in concert with accurate ways of keeping time, of a way to measure longitude, useful for voyagers on ships. Johannes Kepler, the great astronomer of the Holy Roman Empire, wrote in a note to Galileo: "I may perhaps seem rash in accepting your claims so readily with no support of my own experience, but why should I not believe a most learned mathematician, whose very style attests the soundness of his judgment!" As an aside, please note the scientific thought collective in operation even four hundred plus years ago!

I repeat this quote from Kepler because it is very telling not only of Galileo's times, but also of the changes that Copernicus, Galileo, Kepler, Newton, and others ultimately bring to bear on even the current controversy. Let's first, though, finish a brief version of the events in Galileo's story. In 1610, after the book was released, Galileo thought it politic to go to Rome and publicize his discoveries. He had been there once before in 1597 to discuss geometry with Christoph Clavius, the eminent Jesuit mathematician. Now when he returned, with the fame of his book spreading, he was greeted warmly and even received the endorsement of the Collegio Romano, the central institution of the Jesuit educational system. The Vatican regarded Father Clavius, now in his seventies, and his colleagues as the top astronomical authorities in the world, and they were all actively using Galileo's telescopes.

Realize, though, that this world was still an Aristotelian world as interpreted and modified by Thomas Aquinas and deep in the grasp of the Protestant revolution. Aristotle still ranked as the greatest thinker of all time, and the Jesuits were bound to belief in an *unchanging cosmos*. But during Galileo's visit, a social bulletin of the time reported, "On Friday evening of the past week in the *Collegio Romano*, in the presence of cardinals and of the Marquis of Monticelli, its promoter, a Latin oration was recited, with other compositions in praise of Signor Galileo Galilei, mathematician to the grand duke, magnifying and exalting to the heavens his new observation of new planets that were unknown to the ancient philosophers" (qtd. in Sobel 42).

The marquis mentioned is a young Roman named Federico Cesi, who founded the world's first scientific society, the Lyncean Academy (Sobel 42). Cesi pooled his wealth, foresight, and curiosity to establish a forum free from university control or prejudice and made the society international. The lynx was the symbol and source of the name of the group because Cesi saw the importance of studying nature and felt this sharp-eyed cat was the perfect emblem. Galileo was made a member of the Lyncean Academy on that 1610 trip, and later Cesi remained resolutely at his side through the trial(s) and became his publisher.

Galileo also befriended Maffeo Cardinal Barberini, who later became Pope Urban VIII, the pope who charged Galileo with heresy. Until the trial, they were actually good friends and exchanged significant correspondence.

In 1614, Galileo wrote a letter to Grand Duchess Christina of Lorraine, in which he tried to explain to this very devout Catholic lady how one of her favorite passages from Joshua in the Bible could be more easily explained by the Copernican theory of the earth going around the Sun, rather than the Aristotelian/Ptolemaic view of the earth at the center of the universe and the Sun going around it. This letter was to haunt him the rest of his life. Galileo himself, ever the devout Catholic, stated that

> These literary devices had been inserted into the Bible for the sake of the masses, to aid their understanding of matters pertaining to their salvation. In the same way, biblical language had also simplified certain physical effects in Nature, to conform to common experience. Holy Scripture and Nature, are both emanations from the divine word; the former dictated by the Holy Spirit, the latter observant executrix of God's commands. (qtd. in Sobel 63)

Does this sound like a man who didn't have God in his life?

A friend, the Benedictine monk Benedetto Castelli, warned Galileo that the grand duchess was upset by his letter. In a response to Castelli, Galileo wrote

> I believe that the intention of Holy Writ was to persuade men of the truths necessary for salvation, such as neither science nor any other means could render credible, but only the voice of the Holy Spirit. But I do not think it necessary to believe that the same God who gave us our senses, our speech, our intellect, would have put aside the use of these, *to teach us instead such things as with their help we could find out for ourselves, particularly in the case of these sciences of which there is not the smallest mention in the Scriptures.* (qtd. in Sobel 65, italics mine)

Castelli made a number of copies of this letter and shared it with a large number of friends. One year to the day after Galileo wrote to Castelli, he found himself denounced from the pulpit of the Church of Santa Maria Novella, right in his home city of Florence, by Father Thomaso Caccini, a young Dominican with ties to a group of Galileo haters (Sobel 66). Caccini branded all mathematicians in general as "practitioners of diabolical arts . . . enemies of true religion" (qtd. in Sobel 66). Another Dominican submitted a copy of Galileo's widely read letter to an inquisitor general in Rome. Fearing that critical passages might have been altered (which indeed had happened), Galileo submitted a correct copy to a friend at the Vatican, who in turn gave it to a number of cardinals in hopes of clearing Galileo's name.

According to Sobel, at this point (still 1614), Galileo took pains to establish the antiquity of the Sun-centered universe, which dated all the way back to Pythagoras in the sixth century B.C., was later upheld by Plato in his old age and also adopted by Aristarchus of Samos, as reported by Archimedes, before being codified by the Catholic canon Copernicus in 1543. Galileo had good reason to suspect that this theory stood on the verge of suppression and in his letter to the Grand Duchess Christina argued passionately against such action.

Galileo was asking for a distinction to be made between questions of science and articles of faith at a time in history when the Catholic Church was under major assault in western Europe. Shaken and stunned by the Protestant Reformation started in Germany around 1517, the Church took up a very defensive position that lasted throughout the sixteenth and seventeenth centuries, a period Catholics now call the Counter-Reformation. Rome tried vainly to have an ecumenical council for many years, but many political disputes over where and when to hold it postponed its being held.

Finally, Pius III, to whom Copernicus had dedicated his book, convened the Council of Trent. Trent is near the Italian border with the Holy Roman Empire of the German nation. The council met irregularly for eighteen years (1545–63) and ultimately drafted a series of decrees. (The council actually met under three popes.) These decrees dictated how clergy were to be educated and who was empowered to interpret Holy Scripture, declaring in 1546 that "no one, relying on his own judgment and distorting the Sacred Scriptures according to his own conceptions, shall dare to interpret them" (qtd. in Sobel 72). A series of papal bulls were issued in 1564 (the year Galileo was born) and were ultimately formulated into a profession of faith, worded by the Council of Trent, and solemnly sworn over the ensuing decades by Church officials and other Catholics. The profession of faith said,

I most firmly accept and embrace the Apostolic and ecclesiastical traditions and the other observances and constitutions of the Church. I also accept Sacred Scripture in the sense in which it has been held, and is held, by Holy Mother Church, to whom it belongs to judge the true sense and interpretation of the Sacred Scripture, nor will I accept or interpret it in any way other than in accordance with the unanimous agreement of the Fathers. (qtd. in Sobel 72)

Sobel notes that

Galileo's letter to the Grand Duchess indirectly charged his opponents with violating this oath by bending the Bible to their purposes. His opponents, on the other hand, judged Galileo guilty of the same crime. His only hope of winning the argument lay in producing proof positive for the Copernican system. Then since no truth found in Nature could contradict the truth of Scripture, everyone would realize that the father's judgment about the placement of the heavenly bodies had been hasty, and required reinterpretation in the light of scientific discovery. (72)

By early 1618, Galileo returned to Rome having mustered as many arguments as he could, most important of which was his discovery of tidal motions of the great oceans, which he believed bore witness that the planet really did spin through space. "If the earth stood still, then what could make its waters rush to and from, rising and falling at regular intervals along the coasts?" (qtd. in Sobel 74). His writings on the tides were again ahead of his time by at least a century, and he carefully documented them in another book. While in Rome, he argued Copernicus's case at various meetings.

At this point, the pope (Paul V) decided to have his consultors decide once and for all whether Copernican doctrine could be condemned as heretical. The pope summoned his theological adviser, Roberto Cardinal Bellarmino, the preeminent Jesuit intellectual who had served as inquisitor at the trial of Giordano Bruno (another Copernican). Bellarmino was known as the "hammer of heretics." He had once confided to Prince Cesi (remember the Lyncean Society) that he considered the opinion of Copernicus to be heretical and the motion of the earth contrary to the Bible. He himself had studied astronomy at Florence, used

Galileo's own telescope, and highly respected Galileo. The only fault he found with Galileo was his insistence that the Copernican model was a true scenario and not a hypothesis. Further, he said that Galileo should stick to astronomy in public and not try to tell anyone how to interpret the Bible.

At Pope Paul V's request, the cardinals of the Holy Office of the Inquisition framed the Copernican argument as two propositions to be voted on by a panel of eleven theologians:

1. The Sun is the center of the world, and consequently is immobile of local motion; and
2. The Earth is not the center of the world, nor is it immobile, but it moves as a whole and also with diurnal motion. (Sobel 78)

According to Sobel,

The unanimous verdict of the panel pronounced the first idea not only "formally heretical," in that it directly contradicted Holy Scripture, but also "foolish and absurd" in philosophy. The theologians found the second concept equally shoddy philosophically, and "erroneous in faith" meaning that although it did not gainsay the Bible in so many words, it nevertheless undermined a matter of faith. (78)

Galileo was summoned three days later to see Cardinal Bellarmino, who informed Galileo of the decision and admonished him to abandon defending this opinion as fact. Later the same day Father Michelangelo Seghizzi, the Dominican commissary general of the Holy Office of the Inquisition, who had been one of the eleven voting theologians, told Galileo to relinquish the opinion of Copernicus or else the Holy Office would proceed against him. Galileo acquiesced to both demands. Though he stayed in Rome three more months and he met with many people, he made no more public pronouncements at this time. Even Bellarmino noted that though Galileo still held his opinion, he had abjured to the rules and now would treat his view only as a hypothesis, not fact.

There is much more to tell of the story, but suffice it to say that from then (1616) until 1632, Galileo worked on a great number of other things and laid the ground work for Newton and others in the late 1600s to talk about gravity, the tides, and other major discoveries. In fact, in reading Sobel, one sees that Newton, though an equally great thinker, was deeply indebted to Galileo for most of his astronomical findings, including the basics of the laws of gravity.

Many histories say there were two trials of Galileo, but actually there was only one in 1633. The initial confrontation recounted above was not a trial, though it has often been mistakenly reported as one. In 1624, Galileo had approached Pope Urban to let him publish a new book in which he might treat Copernicus hypothetically. Galileo was convinced that he had been given permission, so he started writing his *Dialogue*, in which he had three friends discoursing on scientific matters, one of which was the Copernican ideas. It was finally published in February 1632.

In the spring of 1633, the Inquisition questioned him. Now, realize that he was sixty-nine years old by this time. The first day they grilled him in particular on his earlier conversation with Cardinal Bellarmino and the Dominican commissary general. In this discourse and at his advanced age, Galileo was in agony over his position. Scientifically he was sure Copernicus was right, but in the *Dialogue* he had in fact offered arguments on both sides of the question. In one of his answers, he wrote, "I have neither maintained nor defended in that book the opinion that the Earth moves and that the Sun is stationary but rather have demonstrated the opposite of the Copernican opinion and shown that the arguments of Copernicus are weak and inconclusive" (qtd. in Sobel 253). Galileo never lied under oath. He was a Catholic who had come to believe something Catholics were forbidden to believe. Rather than break with the Church, he had tried to hold—and at the same time not hold—this problematic hypothesis, this image of a mobile earth. That Galileo believed in his own innocence and sincerity is clear from letters he wrote before, during, and long after the trial.

Though this is a longish story, please take note of the parallels with the modern argument. Those Christian sects that interpret the Bible literally are limited in their vision by the exact same quandary. To their way of thinking, to allow evolution to stand as a scientific theory, a prevalent paradigm in which the entire discipline of biology operates, is to undermine the Bible. If evolution is true, then the creation story is at best suspect, and the "godless" people who espouse evolution will ultimately lead to the moral decay of our children and all society.

Consider also who are the "Fathers" cited in the Council of Trent credo. In Galileo's time, the thinking of at least the Western world was dominated by Aristotelian philosophy, which postulated that it was possible to answer all questions through the mind and thought processes. The Church, as the dominant force in western Europe prior to the Reformation, held tightly not only to Aristotle, but to an Aristotle as seen through the eyes of Thomas Aquinas. There was a revolution occurring at the same time, perhaps encouraged by the Reformation, but more so by an increase in technology and distribution of information owing to the printing press. Newton, Kepler, Copernicus, and Galileo demonstrated that observation and experimentation could settle questions concerning natural phenomena. The contributions of the physical scientists promoted a revolution in all thought. As an earth-centered universe gave way to a system of planets centered around the Sun, other changes in thought followed about motion, time, space, and relations between bodies. In fact, it gradually began to seem possible that knowledge gained in this way could surpass and replace that acquired by studies of ancient authorities. Despite the tremendous success of investigators using experiments, the question of how best to obtain new knowledge was still evolving by the time Darwin comes along. "Fathers," churches, and other authoritarian figures were threatened by the notion that intellectuals and even the masses might be able to think for themselves.

With Newton, the scientific method reached new levels of acceptance. It led to new freedom of thought and the incentive to develop new ideas. The real advances in science were promoted by independent and curious men who did original work for the love of learning about nature, and who met together of their own free will to discuss learned subjects. They formed "academies." These academies in the sixteenth and seventeenth centuries were in great conflict with the authoritarian nature of the world. If one looks closely, there are presently still vestiges of the Aristotelian and the authoritative approaches to thinking, and they directly affect the current debate on evolution.

RECENT HISTORY

The current "trial," if I can call it that, wants to pit science against religion again. The demand for equal time in schools was defeated in 1982 in the *Rev. Bill McLean et al. v. Arkansas Board of Education* case. Creationist activists had previously gotten the state of Arkansas to pass Act 590, legislation that required public schools to give "balanced treatment" to what they called "creation science" and "evolution science." This case tested the constitutionality of Act 590. Judge William Overton's final opinion focused on the question of what is science. Overton, drawing from the testimony of Michael Ruse, a philosopher of science at Guelph University, defined science descriptively as "what scientists do" and "what is accepted by the scientific community." But he also incorporated what he called the essential characteristics of science, namely:

1. it is guided by natural law;
2. it has to be explanatory by references to natural law;
3. it is testable against the empirical world;
4. its conclusions are tentative—that is, they are not necessarily the final word;
5. it is falsifiable.

Judge Overton concluded that creation science "fails to meet these essential characteristics" and thus "is not science" (Overton 318). Further, he went on to say that creation science was religious. The case was not primarily a victory for evolutionary theory itself but rather, because of the way it was tried, spoke to deeper philosophical issues about the nature of science and religion and their relation to the law.

Given this case, what might it tell us about the future? Where will evolution, creationism, and Catholicism find themselves in the next millennium?

In the mainline Judaic and Christian religious beliefs, there is no real controversy, though one can find individuals and certain small groups who will not accept all of evolution, particularly the descent of humans from apes. The fundamentalist and evangelical Christian churches, with their literal interpretation of the Bible, continue to reject most versions of evolution, though this rejection also varies from sect to sect and there is much dissention among them. Actually, for scientists defending themselves against attack from these groups, one of the most troubling problems is the myriad of definitions for creationism. They range from the absolute literalists whose faith system affirms that God created the world, all the creatures, and singular man in six days, resting on the seventh, to some creationists who will allow microevolution but not macroevolution. The latter group holds that some changes have occurred in an evolutionary fashion at the cellular level, but denies that any evolution of species to species has ever occurred.

As long as these groups will not understand and accept the difference between science and faith systems, there is little hope of their ever accepting evolution. The intellectual dilemma and the potential consequences, which these people do not recognize, are that in essence they are rejecting all of modern science: in saying evolution is not a valid theory, they reject the whole notion of what is a theory. If they understood their own conundrum, they would also not believe in gravity, string theory, plate tectonics, and so on. Optimistically, one has to hope that in the next millennium, as more of nature and the universe is discovered and elucidated, these individuals will begin to better understand how they can accept these scientific discoveries but be faithful to their beliefs, just as good scientists can be faithful to theirs.

Teilhard de Chardin best stated Catholicism's core ideas on evolution in the 1950s. As a paleontologist, a priest, and a Jesuit, he laid the groundwork for modern Catholicism's free acceptance of evolution, which Pope John Paul II recently reaffirmed. In his seminal work, Teilhard notes that "morphologically the leap was extremely slight" (163). By this, he means that the change in human form (morphology) from the ape body was not a complicated step of evolution. In chapter 1, he discusses in great detail how logically the orderly evolution of hominids occurred.

When water is heated to boiling point under normal pressure, and one goes on heating it, the first thing that follows—without change of temperature—is a tumultuous expansion of freed and vaporised molecules. Or, taking a series of sections from the base towards the summit of a cone, their area decreases constantly; then suddenly, with another infinitesimal displacement, the surface vanishes leaving us with a *point*. Thus by these remote comparisons we are able to imagine the mechanism involved in the critical threshold of reflection.

By the end of the Tertiary era, the psychical temperature in the cellular world had been rising for more than 500 million years. From branch to branch, layer to layer, we have seen how nervous systems followed *pari passu* the process of increased complication and concentration. Finally, with the primates, an instrument was fashioned so remarkably supple and rich that the step immediately following could not take place without the whole animal psychism being as it were recast and consolidated on itself. Now this movement did not stop, for there was nothing in the structure of the organism to prevent it advancing. When the anthropoid, so to speak, had been brought "mentally" to boiling point some further calories were added. Or, when the anthropoid had almost reached the summit of the cone, a final effort took place along the axis.

. . .

Those who adopt the spiritual explanation are right when they defend so vehemently a certain transcendence of man over the rest of nature. But neither are the materialists wrong when they maintain that man is just one further term in a series of animal forms. (Teilhard de Chardin 168–69)

Teilhard goes on to philosophically expand man's evolution into the future as a logical progression from alpha to omega, a progression through the noosphere. This well thought out joining of science, philosophy, and religion has allowed Catholicism not to be troubled by the evolution-creation debate.

So What about the Next Millennium?

As I see it, there is an interesting intersection of the explosion of science and religion that may show us the future clearly. Literary criticism of the Bible is an active phenomenon of the past 70 to 120 years (depending on which Christian religion you want to look at). In many ways, this period is a very short time for an intellectual exercise of this proportion. New interpretations of the meaning and context of the words have allowed many mainstream Christian religions to evaluate and scrutinize carefully where new scientific discoveries intersect with the Bible and its teachings.

To this we should add that since 1940 science has quadrupled its knowledge base and accelerated its technological development. Verification of science is dependent on the skill and sophistication of the technology available at any moment, and the rapid infusion of new technology is changing what have been historical limits to science.

If we continue to widen our knowledge of the nature of the universe at the current ever-accelerating rate, who knows how close science will come to understanding the nature of the "first cause," a God. As we continue to investigate and reinterpret the meaning of our interpretations of God (the Bible for one), what role will science play? Will the next millennium find a greater and greater fusion of science and the "unknown," and in that context will the argument between evolution and creationism go away as trivial and uninteresting? In a poll done in 1997 by Edward Larson of the University of Georgia and published in *Nature*, approximately 40 percent of all working physicists and biologists hold strong spiritual beliefs. Scientists are not ignorant of God and belief systems. Unfortunately, too many creationists are ignorant of science!

My greater fear and prediction is that unless humans come to grips with the fact that they are a natural part of the ecosystem and that as a species they are destroying it at a rate never seen historically, they will, like the dinosaur of sixty-five million years ago, go away in the blink of an eye. Then the ultimate forecast for evolution, creationism, and Catholicism in the next millennium will be moot, for there will be no humans, and Darwinian evolution will then be absolutely verified by our own extinction. At that point, the debate will be silenced because no humans will be around to notice and take cognizance of the reality that we brought the Apocalypse upon ourselves through Darwin's mechanism—natural selection!

Works Cited

Breyer, J. A. "To Reweave a Rainbow: Reflection on the Unity of Knowledge." *Journal of College Science Teaching* (December 1999–January 2000): 148–51.

Bronowski, J. *Science and Human Values*. New York: Harper Torchbooks, 1975.

Fleck, L. *Genesis and Development of a Scientific Fact*. Chicago: University of Chicago Press, 1979.

Malthus, T. *An Essay on the Principle of Population*. 1798. Reprinted as *An Essay on Population*. Introduction by Michael Fogarty. London: Dent, 1958.

Margulis, L. Foreword to *The Spirit in the Gene,* by R. Morrison, viii–ix. Ithaca: Cornell University Press, 1999.

Marx, K., and F. Engels. *The Manifesto of the Communist Party*. Translated by F. Engels. London: Wm. Reeves Book Seller, 1888.

Morrison, R. *The Spirit in the Gene*. Ithaca: Cornell University Press, 1999.

Overton, W. R. "United States District Court Opinion: *McLean v. Arkansas*." In *Tower of Babel*, by R. T. Pennock, 5–6. Cambridge: MIT Press, 1982.

Sagan, C., and A. Druyan. *Shadows of Forgotten Ancestors*. London: Random House, 1992.

Snow, C. P. *The Two Cultures*. Cambridge: Cambridge University Press, 1959.

Sobel, D. *Galileo's Daughter: A Historical Memoir of Science, Faith, and Love*. New York: Walker, 1999.

Teilhard de Chardin, Pierre. *The Phenomenon of Man*. New York: Harper, 1959.

11

The Quest for Christian Unity at the Millennium

Wilburn T. Stancil

INTRODUCTION

On October 31, 1999, Cardinal Edward Cassidy, president of the Pontifical Council for Promoting Christian Unity, and Bishop Christian Krause, president of the Lutheran World Federation, signed the "Joint Declaration on the Doctrine of Justification" at St. Anna's Lutheran Church in Augsburg, Germany. Both the date and the location of the signing are significant. It was on October 31, 1517, that Martin Luther posted his *Ninety-Five Theses,* and it was in the city of Augsburg in 1530 that Emperor Charles V assembled a conference of Martin Luther's followers to draft the Augsburg Confession, one of the founding documents of the Lutheran Church.

The joint declaration signed by Catholics and Lutherans states that the "teaching of the Lutheran churches presented in this declaration does not fall under the condemnations from the Council of Trent" (qtd. in "Lutherans, Roman Catholics," 1). Moments after the historic signing, Pope John Paul II issued a statement calling the document "a milestone on the difficult path to re-establishing full unity among Christians" and a "valuable contribution to the *purification of historical memory* and to our *common witness*" (qtd. in "A Milestone," 4, italics in original).

The ecumenical movement, visibly reflected in the events at Augsburg, can be defined as the attempt to "re-establish full visible unity among all the baptized" (John Paul II, *Ut Unum Sint*, 77). Yet the quest for unity among Christians does not begin with Catholics and Lutherans but rather with Jesus himself, who prayed to the father "that they may all be one so that the world may believe that [the father] has sent me" (John 17:20). It would be difficult to dispute the fact that the disunity of Christianity has done much to mar its witness to the world, but as we begin this new millennium, are Christians any closer to unity?

This chapter explores the status of the Roman Catholic Church's quest for Christian unity through an examination of official Catholic teaching on the subject. Though the Catholic Church has had extensive interreligious dialogue with numerous non-Christian religions, especially Judaism and Islam, the discussion in this chapter is limited to the Catholic Church's ecumenical efforts with other Christian groups.

The commitment of the Roman Catholic Church today to ecumenism is unequivocal and irrevocable. John Paul II has called the ecumenical task "one of the pastoral priorities" of his pontificate (*Ut Unum Sint* 99). Division, the Catholic Church believes, "openly contradicts the will of Christ, provides a stumbling block to the world and inflicts damage on the most holy cause of proclaiming the good news to every creature" (*Unitatis Redintegratio* 1). The unity of all Christians is grounded in the very essence of God as Trinity (John Paul II, *Ut Unum Sint*, 8, 26). Therefore, a correlation exists between the union of the persons of the Godhead and the union of God's people (*Lumen Gentium* 14). Unity is not something added on to the Church but stands at the very essence of what it means to be the people of God (John Paul II, *Ut Unum Sint*, 9).

But how is it that the Church has arrived at such disunity today, and what are the prospects for Christian unity in the new millennium?

HERESY AND SCHISM IN THE EARLY CHURCH

The early Church made no clear distinction between heresy and schism. The Apostle Paul used the words *heresy (hairesis)* and *schism (skisma)* interchangeably to refer to dissentions, factions, and divisions within the Church, especially Eucharistic divisions (1 Corinthians 1:10; 11:18–19; 12:25). Paul considered such divisions to be a product of human sinfulness (Galatians 5:20).

Eventually, however, the Church would in fact distinguish between heresy and schism. Heretics were assumed to be in error in their doctrines, whereas schismatics were assumed to have either divided the Church internally or broken away from the Church, fracturing its unity. The two were never completely separated, however. Augustine considered heresy to be "schism grown old" (cited by Bonner 218).

The problem of Church unity was an acute one from the beginning of Christianity. The many controversies between Jewish and Gentile Christians in the first century demonstrate that unity was forged out of diversity rather than diversity disrupting an original, pristine unity. Nor was this diversity limited to the first century. The competing visions of the message and meaning of the Christian faith spawned theological tensions throughout the early centuries of Christianity. And yet by the fourth century, a broad consensus and unity did emerge, centered in and defined by bishops, creeds, liturgy, and the emerging canon of Scripture. But such unity should not obscure the diversity that existed from the beginning (see Bauer; Hultgren; Turner).

Prior to the legalization of Christianity in A.D. 313, the Church faced the problem of dealing with Christians who lapsed during persecution and later sought to be restored to the Church. Early on, the Western Church stipulated rigorous requirements for the lapsed who wished to reunite with the Church, including in some cases rebaptism (Eusebius 7.2–9). For example, during the persecution under Emperor Decian (A.D. 249–51), Novatian, a priest and theologian, opposed the readmission of the lapsed. When a Roman Synod excommunicated Novatian, he started a schismatic church that lasted into the eighth century (Kelly 472).

Out of the Novatian controversy would come the famous principle stated by Cyprian, bishop of Carthage: *extra ecclesiam nulla salus* (no salvation outside the Church). Cyprian argued that separation from the institutional Church removed one from the sacraments, which were valid only within the institutional Church. Cyprian presided over the Council of Carthage in A.D. 256, which declared that all heretical and schismatic baptisms were ecclesiastically invalid. Only an ecclesiastically valid Church can have valid sacraments. "You cannot have God for your Father if you have not the Church for your mother," stated Cyprian (48–49). Bishop Callistus and the Roman Church rejected this rigorous view in favor of a more compassionate view toward the lapsed.

The same controversy arose again as a result of the persecution under Emperor Diocletian (A.D. 303–5). The Donatists separated from the Catholic Church over whether or not clergy who compromised their faith during persecution retained ecclesiastical authority. Because salvation was found only in the one, holy, catholic, and apostolic Church, Augustine believed that force could be used to compel the Donatists to come into the Church, so long as the force was exercised out of love. Thus, a precedent was set that would continue for the next fifteen hundred years in dealing with both non-Christians and non-Catholic Christians.

The Century Prior to Vatican II

In order to get a clear picture of where the Roman Catholic Church stands in its quest for unity at the millennium, it is instructive to explore the Church's self-understanding and its relationship with non-Catholic Christians for the century prior to Vatican II. To do so, we can explore four papal documents from 1856–1959.

Singulari Quidem

On March 17, 1856, Pope Pius IX addressed the Church in Austria in an allocution entitled *Singulari Quidem*. Condemning the "error of indifferentism" by which all belief systems, religious or secular, are embraced as paths to the truth, Pius IX states:

> There is only one true, holy, Catholic Church, which is the Apostolic Roman Church. There is only one See founded in Peter by the word of the Lord, outside of which we cannot find either true faith or eternal salvation. He who does not have the Church for a mother cannot have God for a father, and whoever abandons the See of Peter on which the Church is established trusts falsely that he is in the Church. Thus, there can be no greater crime, no more hideous stain than to . . . divide the Church. (4.2–5)

Praeclara Gratulationis Publicae

On June 20, 1894, Pope Leo XIII promulgated an encyclical entitled *Praeclara Gratulationis Publicae* (Tokens of Public Rejoicing), which dealt in detail with the reunion of Christendom. The language and tone of the pastoral letter is similar to that of Pius IX's 1856 document to the Church in Austria. For example, Eastern Orthodox Christians are referred to as dissenters "from the Catholic belief" and are admonished to "put an end to their dissentions" and to "return to the fold they have abandoned."

Leo's criticisms of Protestantism are directed at the growing liberalism in Protestantism on the Continent in the late nineteenth century. Thus, he centers his comments on Protestant liberalism's emphasis on naturalism and rationalism in its formulation of Christian doctrines, especially with reference to the divine nature of Christ and the authority of the Bible. The result, according to Leo, is a Protestantism that produces "conflicting opinions and numerous sects."

Mortalium Animos

By the time Pius XI promulgated his encyclical *Mortalium Animos* (Souls of Mortals) on January 6, 1928, the ecumenical situation again was different. In 1910 at Edinburgh, 414 delegates from 122 denominations and forty-three countries gathered to discuss the divisions missionaries faced as they sought to spread Christianity to non-Christian areas of the world. Out of this meeting, the modern ecumenical movement was born, eventually leading to the organization of the World Council of Churches in 1948. From the beginning, Orthodox and Protestant communities were involved in this ecumenical movement, and even though the Catholic Church is still not an official member of the World Council of Churches, in 1958 Catholic theologians became full members of the communion on Faith and Order, an important theological group within the World Council of Churches (Stransky, "Ecumenical Movement," 456–57).

Pius XI's 1928 encyclical, however, is highly critical of this emerging ecumenical movement, noting that such attempts at unity "can nowise be approved by Catholics, founded as they are on that false opinion which considers all religions to be more or less good and praiseworthy" (2). The pontiff refers to ecumenists as "pan-Christians" (4, 9) and to their churches as "assemblies," at one point as "motley assemblies" (7). He affirms that "the Church of Christ not only exists to-day and always, but is also exactly the same as it was in the time of the Apostles" (6.13). For Catholics to involve themselves in the ecumenical movement is to support "false Christianity" and "compromise" (6.8). Citing 2 John 10, "If any man come to you and bring not this doctrine, receive him not," the pope says that this verse forbids "any intercourse with those who professed a mutilated and corrupt version of Christ's teachings" (9). Examples of corrupt teachings include the denial of tradition as a source of revelation, ecclesiastical hierarchy as divinely constituted, transubstantiation, and the veneration of saints.

Pius XI ends the encyclical by stressing that "the union of Christians can only be promoted by promoting the return to the one true Church of Christ of those who are separated from it, for in the past they have unhappily left it" (10). Both Orthodox and Protestants are assured that if they will "humbly beg light from heaven, there is no doubt that they will recognize the one true Church of Jesus Christ" (13).

Ad Petri Cathedram

In the final document, *Ad Petri Cathedram* (To the Chair of Peter), released on June 29, 1959, Pope John XXIII anticipates the new directions that Vatican II would take. The pope interprets the ecumenical movement not as a threat to Catholicism but as "evidence that [non-Catholics] are moved by an intense desire for unity of some kind" (64). He refers to non-Catholic churches as Christian communities, not assemblies, and calls non-Catholic Christians "brethren who are separated from us" (86), not dissenters or pan-Christians. Citing Augustine, John XXIII notes "Whether they wish it or not, they are our brethren. They cease to be our brethren only when they stop saying 'Our Father' " (86).

Although making clear that there is to be no concession to error, falsehood, or vice (95), John XXIII nonetheless invites "all who are not of this fold but reverence and worship God and strive in good faith to obey His commands" to be a part of the Second Vatican Council and the search for unity. "We are not inviting you to a strange home," he notes, "but to your own, to the abode of your forefathers" (84). The pontiff cites the often-stated aphorism: in essentials, unity; in doubtful matters, liberty; in all things, charity (72).

Vatican II

The opening of the Church to the modern world *(aggiornamento)* at the Second Vatican Council brought renewal in many areas, including that of the Church's relationship to other Christian communities. Along with documents in areas of theology and church life, the council also produced a major document on ecumenism, which one writer called "the single most influential document on ecumenism written in the twentieth century" (Kinnamon 144). This decree, *Unitatis Redintegratio* (Restoration of Unity, usually referred to as the Decree on Ecumenism), declares the restoration of unity to be "one of the principal concerns" of the council. Rather than assigning blame for divisions, the decree stresses that division "openly contradicts the will of Christ, scandalizes the world," and damages the preaching of the gospel. Rather than interpreting the ecumenical impulse of the twentieth century as misguided, the decree considers the desire for unity a gift of the Holy Spirit (1).

The Decree on Ecumenism also represents a major shift from the former model of Catholic self-sufficiency, acknowledging that the divided Church is an incomplete Church (Stransky, "Decree on Ecumenism," 401). Its focus is more on the *"restoration* of Christian unity rather than [on] a *return* of non-Catholics to the already-existing unity of the Catholic Church" (McBrien 675, italics in original). Rooted in the council's statement that the Church "subsists" in the Catholic Church, rather than in the notion that the Church "is" the Catholic Church (*Lumen Gentium* 8), the decree acknowledges that "many elements of sanctification and of truth can be found outside her visible structure." Thus, "separated churches and communities, though . . . they suffer from defects, have by no means been deprived of significance and value in the mystery of salvation" (*Lumen Gentium* 8), although the fullness of grace and truth exists in the Catholic Church.

The Declaration on Religious Liberty *(Dignitatis Humanae)*, another important document from Vatican II, provides additional context for the Church's evolving view on unity. The declaration states that

> Truth is to be sought after in a manner proper to the dignity of the human person and his social nature. The inquiry is to be free, carried on with the aid of teaching or instruction, communication and dialogue. In the course of these, people explain to one another the truth they have discovered, or think they have discovered, in order thus to assist one another in the quest for truth. Moreover, as the truth is discovered, it is by a personal assent that individuals are to adhere to it. (3)

In other words, truth cannot depend on coercion for its progress.

Highlights of the Decree on Ecumenism include:

- Catholics and non-Catholics are both to blame for divisions (*Unitatis Redintegratio* 3).
- Non-Catholics born into other Christian communities today cannot be charged with the sin of separation (3).
- Baptized non-Catholics are incorporated into Christ and therefore should be called Christians and accepted as brothers by the Catholic Church, even though their communion with the Catholic Church is an "imperfect communion" (3).
- Many of the "elements and endowments" that build up the life of the Church, such as the Word of God, the life of grace, and gifts of the Spirit, "can exist outside the visible boundaries of the Catholic Church" (3).
- All expressions, judgments, and actions should be avoided that do not represent non-Catholics with truth and fairness (4). For example, church history should not be taught polemically but rather "exactly as possible with the facts" (10).

- Although the work of ecumenism includes dialogue among competent experts, ultimately all the Catholic faithful are "to take an active and intelligent part" in ecumenical work (4, but see also 5).
- Catholics should give special attention to the manner in which they present Catholic doctrine, remembering that there exists in Catholic doctrine a "hierarchy of truths" (11).
- The "primary duty" of Catholics is to "make a careful and honest appraisal of whatever needs to be renewed and done in the Catholic household itself." This theme of interior conversion is pervasive and profound throughout the document. The decree refers to this interior conversion as a "spiritual ecumenism," which forms the "soul of the whole ecumenical movement" and includes "change of heart and holiness of life, along with public and private prayer for the unity of Christians" (80).
- The Catholic Church has a special relationship with the Eastern Churches, who, though separated from Rome, are said to possess true sacraments and true apostolic succession. Unlike the case with Protestants, where common worship (*communicatio in sacris*) is discouraged (8), the decree encourages some common worship with Eastern Churches (15). The decree also considers the diversity of customs, observances, and theological formulations in the Eastern Churches to be a prerequisite for and not an obstacle to union.
- In ecumenical relationships, there can be no "false irenicism." Ecumenical activity "cannot be other than fully and sincerely Catholic, that is, loyal to the truth we have received from the Apostles and the Fathers, and in harmony with the faith which the Catholic Church has always professed" (24).

Since Vatican II, the Pontifical Council for Promoting Christian Unity, which John XXIII established in 1960, has been responsible for promoting and engaging in ecumenical dialogue with numerous Christian groups and has issued a number of helpful documents expanding on the principles outlined in the Decree on Ecumenism.

JOHN PAUL II AND *UT UNUM SINT*

The most important Roman Catholic statement on ecumenism since Vatican II is John Paul II's 1995 encyclical *Ut Unum Sint* (That All May Be One). This remarkable document, subtitled *On Commitment to Ecumenism*, reiterates the Vatican II call for ecumenical renewal and encourages "the efforts of all who work for the cause of unity" (3).

In continuity with the Vatican II focus on "spiritual ecumenism," John Paul II calls for inner conversion, which alone can result in "purification of past memories"(*Ut Unum Sint* 2). He especially highlights the spiritual discipline of prayer. "If Christians, despite their divisions, can grow ever more united in common prayer around Christ, they will grow in the awareness of how little divides them in comparison to what unites them" (22). He urges all Christian communities to be drawn into a "spiritual space" so as to hear the voice of Christ in overcoming the obstacles to unity (82–83).

In the encyclical, John Paul II gives careful attention to the ways in which doctrinal formulations are expressed in a given community. He observes that the truths that the Church intends to teach through dogmatic formulas are often expressed in concepts suitable for a specific time frame. Therefore, "intolerant polemics and controversies have made incompatible assertions out of what was really the result of two different ways of looking at the same reality" (38). This principle of taking into account the intention and time frame of doctrinal formulation would be important for ecumenical efforts such as the "Joint Declaration on the Doctrine of Justification" signed by Catholics and Lutherans in 1999.

John Paul II also calls for a "broadening of vocabulary" when referring to Protestants, with a corresponding "significant change in attitudes": "The very expression 'separated brethren' tends to be replaced today by expressions which more readily evoke the deep communion—linked to the baptismal character—which the Spirit fosters in spite of historical and canonical divisions. Today we speak of 'other Christians,' 'others who have received baptism' and 'Christians of other communities' " (42).

The most controversial section of the document concerns the

office of the papacy. In speaking of his role as the "servant of the servants of God" *(servus servorum Dei)*, John Paul II states his openness to "find a way of exercising the primacy which, while in no way renouncing what is essential to its mission, is nonetheless open to a new situation" (95). He invites Church leaders and theologians to dialogue with him on this subject, an offer that Catholics, Orthodox, and Protestants alike have taken up.

CONCLUDING OBSERVATIONS

Ecumenism has a high priority with the Roman Catholic Church today and has especially been a hallmark of the pontificate of John Paul II. Real progress has been made toward the goal of unifying all Christians. However, much remains to be done. In thinking of the challenges that remain, the following matters are important.

First, Catholics must make a commitment to both unity and truth. On the one hand, there can be no settling for "apparent solutions" or trimming the truth (John Paul II, *Ut Unum Sint*, 79). John Paul II has said that "it is not a question of altering the deposit of faith, changing the meaning of dogmas, eliminating essential words from them, accommodating truth to the preferences of a particular age or suppressing certain articles of the Creed under the false pretext that they are no longer understood today. The unity willed by God can be attained only by the adherence of all to the content of the revealed faith in its entirety" (*Ut Unum Sint* 18).

On the other hand, John Paul II also cautions Catholics against a "halfhearted commitment to unity and, even more, a prejudicial opposition or a defeatism which tends to see everything in negative terms" (*Ut Unum Sint* 79). Therefore, the commitment expected of Catholics is dual: to both truth and unity.

Second, the relationship between the Catholic Church and the Orthodox Church continues to be both encouraging and discouraging. On December 7, 1965, Pope Paul VI and Athenagoras I, the Ecumenical Patriarch of Constantinople, met and declared their desire to erase from memory the mutual sentences of excommunication that had become symbolic of the schism between the two Churches since 1054. Since then, however, with the strengthening of the Orthodox Church in Russia and in other former communist nations, ancient controversies have resurfaced concerning doctrines, territorial expansion, and the presence of Eastern Rite Catholics in areas traditionally Orthodox.

John Paul II has especially focused on recapturing for the third millennium the unity that existed between East and West during the first millennium. On May 2, 1995, he promulgated an encyclical *(Orientale Lumen)* that warmly praises the contributions of the Eastern Churches to the faith, while avoiding polemical issues. Elsewhere he invokes a favorite image, calling for the Church to breath with "her two lungs" *(Ut Unum Sint* 54).

Third, the changing face of Protestantism in the United States today presents unique challenges to ecumenism for Catholics. Many of the issues dividing Catholics and Protestants are the same ones that have always divided these two communities of faith—the relationship between Scripture and tradition, the nature of the Eucharist, the role of the Magisterium, and so on. The changes that Vatican II brought about in the 1960s unfortunately coincided exactly with the numerical decline of mainline Protestantism in the United States and with the rapid growth of Evangelical forms of Protestantism. Thus, the timing could hardly be worse for finding common ground on difficult issues.

For example, the fastest growing denominations in the United States today are groups such as the Mormons, Jehovah's Witnesses, Seventh Day Adventists, and Evangelicals such as Southern Baptists, Nazarenes, Pentecostals, and others. On crucial theological issues such as baptism, Eucharist, ministry, and even salvation, these groups have the least in common with the Catholic vision of Christianity. Evidence of this difference can be seen in a statement Reverend Albert Mohler, president of the Southern Baptist Theological Seminary and frequent guest on Larry King Live, recently made. Reverend Mohler declared Roman Catholics to be the object of "spiritual concern and evangelistic mission" for Southern Baptists (Mohler 5). This kind of triumphalism rightfully raises questions in the minds of Catholics concerning the possibility of mutual understanding with Evangelicals.

Interestingly, however, a kind of "ecumenism in the trenches"

(Neuhaus 93) has simultaneously taken place, creating unlikely theological bedfellows. Thus, Evangelicals and Catholics have joined arms in issues such as the pro-life movement, support for school vouchers, family values, and charismatic renewal, and they have even produced two unofficial joint statements, "Evangelicals and Catholics Together" and "The Gift of Salvation." However, based on criticism many Evangelical leaders have received from their own people for signing these two documents, it is clear that many if not most Evangelicals hold the Roman Catholic Church in suspicion.

Mainline Protestantism, on the other hand, which traditionally has had more in common with the Catholic Church, not only has dramatically declined in membership but has erected new barriers to unity, from the Catholic perspective, through its position on such issues as the ordination of women, issues of sexuality, and abortion rights.

Fourth, the spiritual mobility of Americans presents unique problems for Catholic ecumenism. In the United States, where brand loyalty is fast becoming a thing of the past, people often shop for churches the same way they shop for a new TV. That is, "Where can I get the best product that meets my needs for the least investment?" Such comparative shopping has produced a steady decline in denominational loyalty, resulting in either spirituality without institutional religion or church and denominational hopping. This circulation of members occurs in all directions, even with Churches that have much in common with the Roman Catholic Church.

For example, Catholics sometimes become mainline Protestants because they think the Catholic Church is too conservative, or mainline Protestants sometimes become Catholics because they think the mainline Protestant Churches are too liberal, or Catholics and Protestants become Orthodox because they think the Orthodox Church is the true, unchanged, and unchanging Church (See Gillquist; Madrid; Webber).

Such playing of musical chairs among churchgoers has done little to foster ecumenism. In fact, oftentimes it has produced the opposite reaction. The old saying "there's no zeal like that of a convert" is relevant here. In recent years, a new group of "catholic apologists" (Rausch 5) has arisen whose mission is not to promote dialogue with Protestants but to convert them. Many of these apologists are converts themselves to Catholicism from Protestantism, such as Peter Kreeft of Boston College, Thomas Howard of St. John's Seminary, and Scott Hahn of the Franciscan University of Steubenville.

As Peter Huff has noted, the approach of these new apologists "to other Christian communities is more often polemical than irenic. Rather than seeking to find areas of agreement, as official Catholic ecumenism does, they tend to reject mainline Protestantism, not just for its contemporary pluralism and embrace of modernity, but also in some of its foundational doctrines" (cited in Rausch 7). These Catholic apologists are antiecumenical because they obscure the "the extent to which they share a common faith with their Protestant brothers and sisters" (Rausch 7).

However, in defense of these "new apologists," Protestantism has often misunderstood if not misrepresented the Roman Catholic Church, and one can sympathize with the intent to eradicate misunderstandings, even if the effort is at times overzealous.

Finally, Christian unity is a mark of the one, holy, catholic, and apostolic Church. It is both a gift and a task. As a gift, it is grounded in the union of the Persons of the Godhead with God's people (*Lumen Gentium* 14). Thus, as John Paul II notes, "what separates us as believers in Christ is much less than what unites us" (*Crossing the Threshold of Hope* 146). As a task, however, the road is long and difficult, and the obstacles are many. And so, perhaps ultimately it is appropriate that since Vatican II, the Catholic Church has given priority to spiritual ecumenism. Prayer may be in fact the only thing that can ultimately unite all Christians, bringing to fruition the prayer of Jesus "that they all might be one."

WORKS CITED

Bauer, Walter. *Orthodoxy and Heresy in Earliest Christianity*. Philadelphia: Fortress, 1971.

Bonner, Gerald. "Schism and Church Unity." In *Early Christianity: Origins and Evolution to A.D. 600*, edited by Ian Hazlett, 218–28. Nashville: Abingdon, 1991.

Cyprian. *The Unity of the Catholic Church*. Translated and annotated by Maurice Bevenot. New York: Newman, 1956.

Dignitatis Humanae. December 7, 1965.

Eusebius. *Ecclesiastical History*. London: Penguin, 1965.

"Evangelicals and Catholics Together: The Christian Mission in the Third Millennium." *First Things* 43 (May 1994): 15–22.

"The Gift of Salvation." *First Things* 79 (January 1998): 20–23.

Gillquist, Peter E., ed. *Coming Home: Why Protestant Clergy Are Becoming Orthodox*. Ben Lomond, Calif.: Conciliar, 1992.

Hultgren, Arland J. *The Rise of Normative Christianity*. Minneapolis: Fortress, 1994.

John XXIII. *Ad Petri Cathedram*. June 29, 1959.

John Paul II. *Crossing the Threshold of Hope*. New York: Alfred A. Knopf, 1994.

———. *Orientale Lumen*. May 2, 1995.

———. *Ut Unum Sint*. May 30, 1995.

"Joint Declaration on the Doctrine of Justification." Available at: http://www.elca.org, or http://www.vatican/va/.

Kelly, D. F. "Novatian." In *New Dictionary of Theology*, edited by Sinclair B. Ferguson, David F. Wright, and J. I. Packer, 472. Downers Grove, Ill.: InterVarsity, 1988.

Kinnamon, Michael. "Ecumenism." In *A New Handbook of Christian Theology*, edited by Donald W. Musser and Joseph L. Price, 142–45. Nashville: Abingdon, 1992.

Leo XIII. *Praeclara Gratulationis Publicae*. June 20, 1894.

Lumen Gentium. November 21, 1964.

"Lutherans, Roman Catholics Overcome Historic Condemnations." November 4, 1999: 1–8. Available at: http://www.elca.org.

Madrid, Patrick, ed. *Surprised by Truth: 11 Converts Give the Biblical and Historical Reasons for Becoming Catholic*. San Diego: Basilica, 1994.

McBrien, Richard P. *Catholicism*. San Francisco: Harper and Row, 1981.

"A Milestone on the Ecumenical Path." *L'Osservatore Romano*, November 3, 1999: 4–5. Available at: http://www.vatican/va/.

Mohler, R. Albert. "The Southern Baptist Convention and the Issue of Interdenominational Relationships." February 21,

2000: 1–8. Available at: http://www.sbts.edu/mohler/fidelitas/sbcandecumenism.html.

Neuhaus, Richard John. "The Public Square." *First Things* 96 (October 1999): 93.

Pius IX. *Singulari Quidem*. March 17, 1856.

Pius XI. *Mortalium Animos*. January 6, 1928.

Rausch, Thomas P. "The Third Stage of the Ecumenical Movement: Is the Catholic Church Ready?" *Ecumenical Trends* 26 (November 1997): 1–7. Available at: http://www.bu.edu/sth/BTI/ecudocs/rausch.htm.

Stransky, Thomas F. "Decree on Ecumenism." In *Encyclopedia of Catholicism*, edited by Richard P. McBrien, 401–2. San Francisco: HarperCollins, 1995.

———. "Ecumenical Movement." In *Encyclopedia of Catholicism*, edited by Richard P. McBrien, 456–57. San Francisco: HarperCollins, 1995.

Turner, H. E. W. *The Pattern of Christian Truth: A Study in Relations between Orthodoxy and Heresy in the Early Church*. London: A. R. Mowbray, 1954.

Unitatis Redintegratio. November 21, 1964.

Webber, Robert E. *Evangelicals on the Canterbury Trail: Why Evangelicals Are Attracted to the Liturgical Church*. Waco, Tex.: Word, 1985.

AFTERWORD

Poet William Wordsworth once wrote that in our lives there are "spots of time" that retain a "renovating virtue" *(The Prelude)*. Perhaps the transition to the third Christian millennium is one of those "spots of time," and perhaps it can even provide a distinct opportunity for "renovating virtue."

The Roman Catholic Church cannot but be affected by the transformation of cultures that is overwhelming us today. We may, when we are bold, think we can manage this sea change, but why is it happening so *fast*? Deeply embedded in human culture and cultures, as the Church should and needs to be, what stance will it take in the face of the immense and often uneven changes that are occurring worldwide?

It would be so easy to bemoan our fate. Simply to retreat to the comforts and sureties of the past would be as effective as French prelates trying to hold back democracy in the nineteenth century. For the Church to (re)act in a similar way at this time would not only be ineffective and harmful to the people of God, but also a betrayal of its intellectual and cultural tradition, a tradition that long ago encountered the culture and power of Rome, embraced what was good in it, inculturated itself within it, and, bringing its own insights and passions, ultimately "baptized" it.

It is much more difficult, but so much more satisfying, to face the future that is upon us each day with a confidence based on faith that we are partners with a loving God who labors with us to bring about a better world. Such confidence is also based on an intellectual tradition that reaches back over millennia of cultural changes and challenges. This tradition can teach us today and bring us hope.

Some forty years ago, Blessed Angelo Roncalli (Pope John XXIII) encouraged us to open windows to the spirit of the times, to welcome the breath of God. The result was Vatican II. It may

be that the breath of God has become a whirlwind that, per-
chance, has even broken a few windows. Can we, as we steady
ourselves against the gale, say "Welcome"?

Indeed, "a spot of time." Indeed, a time of "renovating virtue." Indeed—recalling the old Chinese curse—interesting times
for a Catholic university.

JOHN J. CALLAHAN, S.J.
Director of Jesuit Mission and Values
Rockhurst University

ABOUT THE AUTHORS

Joseph A. Cirincione is a professor in the Department of English at Rockhurst University, where he has taught for twenty-two years. He teaches a variety of literature and writing courses, specializing in British literature of the Restoration and eighteenth century as well as the romantic period. Dr. Cirincione has taught many courses and presented and published a number of papers on business writing. He is presently at work on a text about business report writing based on psycholinguistic theories of language and reading.

Laura E. Fitzpatrick is an associate professor of economics at Rockhurst University, where she has taught for eight years. She received a Ph.D. in economics from the University of Notre Dame. Social justice and ethical analysis are mainstays in the economics and interdisciplinary business courses she teaches. Dr. Fitzpatrick's research focuses on food security, development, and pedagogy.

Curtis L. Hancock is a professor of philosophy at Rockhurst University and holds the Joseph M. Freeman Chair of Philosophy. He is the president of the American Maritain Association and the Gilson Society for the Advancement of Christian Philosophy. He has coauthored a book on the philosophy of religion, *Truth and Religious Belief* (with Brendan Sweetman), and a book on ethics, *How Should I Live?* (with Randolph Feezell), and has coedited a book on political philosophy, *Freedom, Virtue, and the Common Good* (with Anthony Simon).

Richard J. Janet is an associate professor in the Department of History at Rockhurst University, where he has taught courses in the history of modern Europe since 1985. He received a Ph.D. in history from the University of Notre Dame in 1984. His research interests focus on the religious history of Victorian England. Dr.

Janet currently serves as interim associate dean in the College of Arts and Sciences at Rockhurst.

Wilfred LaCroix, S.J., is an associate professor in the Department of Philosophy at Rockhurst University. Father LaCroix has published on social justice and international justice. His books include *Ethical Principles for Business, War, and International Ethics* and *Patterns, Values, and Horizons: An Ethic.*

Timothy L. McDonald is an associate professor of music and chair of the Department of Communication and Fine Arts at Rockhurst University. He directs the university's choral ensembles as well as Musica Sacra of Kansas City Chorus and Orchestra. Dr. McDonald has served as a director and minister of music at Catholic parishes in New Jersey and Pennsylvania. He has published *John Hothby: La Calliopea Legale* and a variety of articles, and is the classical music writer for Sun Newspapers.

Robert J. Mahoney is a priest of the Kansas City–St. Joseph Catholic Diocese. He is a professor of sociology and chair of the Sociology Department at Rockhurst University. Father Mahoney's professional interests include current social issues and American values. He is especially interested in the interplay between social theory and philosophy as applied to cultural values and social behavior. He has presented papers to a variety of professional societies, including the Association for the Sociology of Religion, the Society for the Scientific Study of Religion, the Religious Research Association, and the American Society of Criminology. With undergraduate degrees in philosophy (St. Benedict's) and theology (Gregorian University, Rome), he also received an M.A. and a Ph.D. in sociology from the University of Missouri–Columbia. His most recent publication reported on an eight-year ethnographic study of nursing home care and end-of-life issues.

Gerald L. Miller holds the John J. and Laura J. Sullivan Chair in Business Ethics at Rockhurst University and is the former director of the Institute of Social Ethics. He has been a Schmitt Fellow (University of Notre Dame), a General Electric Fellow (University of Chicago), and a United Telecom Fellow (Rockhurst University). Professor Miller has also held the George and Gladys

Miller Chair in Business at Rockhurst University. A professor of economics, he received an M.A. and a Ph.D. in economics from the University of Notre Dame.

Wilburn T. Stancil is an associate professor of theology at Rockhurst University and the director of the Rockhurst University Press. He has published more than one hundred chapters in books and articles in journals, most recently in the Dominican journal *New Blackfriars*. Dr. Stancil is a licensed lay preacher in the Episcopal Church.

Brendan Sweetman is an associate professor of philosophy and the chair of the Department of Philosophy at Rockhurst University. He is the coauthor of *Truth and Religious Belief*, coeditor of *Contemporary Perspectives on Religious Epistemology*, and editor of *The Failure of Modernism*, as well as author of numerous articles and reviews in a number of journals and collections in the areas of philosophy of religion and contemporary European philosophy.

Richard E. Wilson is a professor of biology at Rockhurst University, where he has taught for twenty-nine years and been chair of the Division of Sciences for twenty-five years. He teaches evolution each fall to a mixture of both majors and nonmajors, along with honors general biology and physiology. He has been very active in K–12 outreach work, trying to increase the quality of science taught in the Kansas City metro area and particularly to increase the number of students entering into science, mathematics, and engineering. Dr. Wilson has also been active on the national scene working to improve biology curricula and to foster greater understanding of the importance of evolution to modern biology.

INDEX